CITIZEN OF THE WORLD

Essays on Thomas Paine

Edited by Ian Dyck

ST. MARTIN'S PRESS
New York

First published in the United States of America in 1988

Printed in Great Britain

ISBN 0-312-01300-0

Library of Congress Cataloging-in-Publication Data

Citizen of the world: essays on Thomas Paine / edited by Ian Dyck,
    p.   cm.
    Bibliography: p.
    Includes index.
    ISBN 0-312-01300-0 : $29.95
    1. Paine, Thomas, 1737-1809.   2. Revolutionists—United States—
Biography.   3. Political scientists—United States—Biography.
I. Dyck, Ian.
JC178.V2C57   1988
320.5'1'0924—dc19

Contents

To the memory of George

Notes on Contributors

George Spater (1909-84) was formerly Chief Executive Officer of American Airlines. After his retirement in 1973 he was appointed a senior research fellow at Sussex University. He was the author of two books: *William Cobbett: The Poor Man's Friend* (1982) and (with Ian Parsons) *A Marriage of True Minds: An Intimate Portrait of Leonard and Virginia Woolf* (1977).

J.F.C. Harrison is recently retired as Professor of History at Sussex University. He is now engaged in full-time research and writing. Among his several books are *The Second Coming: Popular Millenarianism, 1780-1850* (1979) and *The Common People* (1984).

Joel H. Wiener is Professor of History at the City College of the City University of New York. His publications include *The War of the Unstamped* (1969) and *Radicalism and Freethought in Nineteenth Century Britain: The Life of Richard Carlile* (1983). He is now at work on a life of William Lovett.

Ian Dyck is Assistant Professor of History at St Thomas More College, the University of Saskatchewan, Canada. He did his doctorate in history at Sussex University and is currently preparing a study of the cultural association between William Cobbett and the English farm worker.

Preface

Two and a half centuries ago, at Thetford in the county of Norfolk, was born Thomas Paine, the son of a craftsman. For all appearances the boy Thomas was without great destiny. He had neither wealth nor profound formal education; in the social demography of the poet Thomas Gray he was another inconspicuous enlistment in 'the short and simple annals of the poor'.

The first half of Paine's life of seventy-two years was spent in gaining a marginal living, first as a struggling artisan, then as an exciseman, and briefly as a tobacconist. At Lewes in Sussex during the extra-parliamentary political debates of the 1760s, he acquired some local notice as a 'village Hampden', arguing the Whig case for the rights of Parliament against those of the Crown. In 1774, without fame or fortune, he relocated to America, where suddenly, and without recourse to the established avenues of political or literary apprenticeship, he burst forth with his pamphlet *Common Sense* to become the leading propagandist of the American Revolutionary War. Returning to England in 1787 he became embroiled in European radical politics, authoring in 1791 the first part of his highly influential treatise *Rights of Man* — the most important contemporary English-language defence of the French Revolution. Translating thought into action, Paine took up residence in France itself, where he took a direct hand in the volatile political processes of the Revolution. For the second time within two decades Paine was a leader of national insurrection; as he wrote to President Washington in 1789, 'A share in two revolutions is living to some purpose.'

Paine was arguably the most popular and influential trans-atlantic Radical of the final quarter of the eighteenth century. And yet, as the next century loomed, his name suddenly became synonymous with blasphemy and treason, ostensibly because of his religious heresies. Paine's final decade would be spent in great infamy, and he would die in exile, unnoticed by the world, in 1809.

The life and times of Paine have several times been charted, most recently in a biography by the American historian David Hawke, and in a popular study by the English author, David Powell. Important problems remain to be explored, however, especially with regard to Paine's religious and political orientation in America. More thought should also be lent to the nature of Paine's association with his political (and sometimes free-thinking) allies and successors, most notably Thomas Jefferson, Benjamin Franklin, Richard Carlile and William Cobbett. Lastly, there is the greatly neglected subject of Paine's hostile reception, both public and academic, in the nineteenth and twentieth centuries.

This collection of essays has its focus on these outstanding themes and problems. The volume is inspired and partly based upon the writings and research materials of George Spater, who began research for a book on Paine after publishing his masterful two-volume biography of Cobbett in 1982. The sudden death of Mr Spater in 1984 left his Paine project incomplete, but not unsalvageable, and I have here attempted to assemble, edit and document a set of five chapters (including the Introduction) from Mr Spater's notes and manuscripts. In Chapters 1 through 3 I have bridged periodic gaps in the manuscript with brief commentaries of my own; the Introduction and the concluding chapter appear largely as I found them, with the application of only minor editorial surgery.

Save for the final chapter on Paine's legacy, Part II of the volume consists of essays on Paine by friends and academic associates of Mr Spater. Professor J.F.C. Harrison views Paine within the context of eighteenth- and nineteenth-century millenarian radicalism; Professor Joel Wiener examines the association between Paine and his English publisher and disciple, Richard Carlile; while my own essay explores the

intellectual and cultural liaison between Paine and his erst-
while ideological mentor, William Cobbett.

If only out of loyalty to Paine's own style and meaning,
this volume is addressed equally to the reading public and to
an academic audience. Both communities have contributed to
our understanding of Paine; if the latter has done more with
Paine's political thought, the former has spearheaded enquiry
into the relevance of Paine's secularism to the twentieth
century. Finally, as the title of the volume suggests, the focus
here is not national, for Paine's foremost achievement was to
promote political and religious dissent in three countries on
two continents.

The preparation of this volume has been greatly assisted by
Mrs Hope Spater, who welcomed my intrusion into her home
while I sorted through the manuscripts of her late husband. I am
grateful to St Thomas More College and the University of
Saskatchewan for contributing towards my travel and research
expenses. I would also like to thank Professor J.F.C. Harrison
for providing me with timely editorial advice, and Colleen
Fitzgerald for her assistance with the preparation of the Index.

Ian Dyck
St Thomas More College
University of Saskatchewan

Introduction:
Thomas Paine — Questions for the Historian

George Spater

Several years ago, when I was living in England, I attended a symposium in Brighton on the subject of biography. The participants were all well-established professionals. C.V. Wedgewood presided, the author of distinguished works on Cromwell, Charles I, Montrose and Strafford, to name a few. The others included Susan Chitty, whose most recent biography was about Gwen John, sister of Augustus John. There was Jasper Ridley, author of lives of Palmerston and Wolsey. And the fourth was the handsome Antonia Fraser, who manages to turn out a good biography every other year it seems. I cannot resist adding, for the edification of my fellow Americans, that the paid attendance at this event in the town of Brighton — a town with a population of less than 200,000 — completely filled the meeting room, which held 400 or 500 people, and dozens of would-be attendants were turned away. I cannot imagine anything like that happening at a comparable location in America.

During the question period at the end of the symposium, someone in the audience asked how each of the four writers began work on a biography. Three of them replied that the first thing they did was to make a chronology. Antonia

Fraser, the last to reply, said that her first step was to write down the questions that had to be answered. For the past several years, as I have been digging into the facts pertaining to Thomas Paine, preparatory to writing a life of him, I have frequently come back to this extremely useful approach: What are the questions?

It is true that a chronology is an essential for any biography or for any history, but equally clearly a good biography or a good history cannot be written unless the author identifies the questions that are critical to an understanding of the subject, and attempts to answer those questions.

In the case of every biography there are at least two set questions: what is the person written about really like? That is the first one. And the biographer, in turn, has the problem of deciding how he can present the picture. Is it done through something akin to an essay or series of essays in which the biographee's character is analysed by the author posing as God, or is it done by presenting episodes from the subject's life which allow the reader to see for himself the character of the biographee? Or is it done by some combination of the two?

A second set question in every biography is what should go in and what should be left out? Nothing is more deadly than a biography in which the author puts in everything he knows about his subject. What are the *essential* facts? What do you do with gossip and folklore and myths? Some are so delicious that they become difficult to resist.

George Steiner has argued strenuously that the length of a biography should be dictated by the importance of the subject. I think that is going too far, but Steiner's view supports the conclusion that far more biographies are ruined by being too long than by being too short. Length is no virtue; more often than not it is a curse.

In addition to these set questions that face all authors, regardless of subject, there are always specific questions pertaining to specific biographees, and these are the most important. Paine's life provides some vivid illustrations. He came to America in 1774. He was 37 years old. He was armed with a letter of introduction from Benjamin Franklin who was then acting as London agent for the colony of Pennsylvania.

The introduction said that Paine was 'very capable' of performing work as 'a clerk, or assistant tutor in a school, or assistant surveyor'.[1] Yet, for reasons unknown to us — and Paine seemed to prefer that the countless mysteries surrounding him remain mysteries — he turned his back on the professions of which he was 'very capable', and became a journalist, a profession in which, according to his own statement, he had absolutely *no* experience. Within a few months after his arrival in Philadelphia he was editor, or assistant editor, of a monthly magazine. And in January 1776, after he had been in the country just over a year, he produced what may be his greatest work, a pamphlet entitled *Common Sense* which urged the people of the American colonies to declare their independence. This pamphlet had a tremendous impact on the colonists. Over 100,000 copies were sold to a population of two and half million, the equivalent of ten million copies in today's population. Paine's contemporary, the English-born General Charles Lee, said that Paine 'burst forth upon the world like Jove in thunder'.[2] Page Smith, more nearly our contemporary, wrote that *Common Sense* was 'undoubtedly the most influential pamphlet in American history'.[3] Jefferson wrote that 'No writer has exceeded Paine in ease and familiarity of style; in perspicuity of expression, happiness of elucidation, and in simple and unassuming language.'[4]

This leads naturally to one of the key questions: Paine claimed that before coming to America he had never 'published a syllable in England'; that 'It was the cause of America that made me an author.'[5] A letter in the papers of the Earl of Dartmouth written in 1777 states unequivocally, but without supporting evidence, that Paine had been a 'Grub Street Writer' in London before migrating to America.[6] Is it possible that a man with little formal education, who had never published anything before, could begin a writing career at the age of 37? Nor was this any sort of writing, it was writing on a level unsurpassed by the educated literary stylists of England and America.

I have asked dozens of people this question, and still do not feel satisfied that I have found the correct answer. A few years ago a gentleman in England thought he had found the answer. He announced that he had discovered 'more than forty varied articles' written by Paine that had appeared in the local newspaper published in Lewes, Sussex, where Paine had lived from 1768 to 1774.[7] They were signed '*A* Forester', and we know that several articles Paine later published in America were signed '*The* Forester'. I was very excited by the discovery and took a look at the English paper in which they appeared. Fortunately, or unfortunately, I read beyond the point where the discoverer had stopped, and I found an article in that paper seventeen years later which announced that 'On Tuesday last, after a few days' illness, died, the Rev. Richard Nichell, of East-Dean, author of the many letters that have appeared in this paper, under the signature of "A Forester . . ."'[8]

Of course it is possible that Paine wrote voluminously in England, even if not these articles, but never published anything. Yet such a conclusion would be wholly inconsistent with the compulsive need to publish that Paine manifested throughout the rest of his life. Paine even insisted on publishing articles which his friends urged him to tear up, and was furious when any newspaper editor failed to publish one of his submissions.

Common Sense was by no means a one-shot success. He followed it with the several numbers of the *Crisis* series in which appeared the immortal line 'These are the times that try men's souls'. Thousands upon thousands of other authors who have been writing all their lives are never able to hit upon phrases that became an acknowledged part of the language. And there were many other such happy expressions: 'We have it in our power to begin the world over again'. 'Now is the seed-time of continental union, faith and honor.' 'Government, like dress, is the badge of lost innocence'.[9]

As a result of these writings, Paine occupied an extraordinary position in the hierarchy of the American Revolution, a position in political society no other journalist has ever attained. Paine, never modest about his powers, put it very squarely in 1792: 'I have arrived at an eminence in political literature, the most difficult of all lines to exceed and excel in, which aristocracy, with all its aids, has not been able to reach or rival'.[10] Beveridge, in his *Life of John Marshall*, claims that the only men of his time as well known as Paine in America were Washington, Franklin, Jefferson and that wild patriot,

Patrick Henry.[11] A regiment of the American army celebrating the fourth of July in 1783 toasted: 'the United States & their Congress, the general and army of the United States, and the Congress of the year 1776 and common Sence [*sic*]'.[12] In 1786, at a birthday celebration for Ben Franklin in Philadelphia, the three individuals toasted were 'Dr. Franklin', 'General Washington' and 'Thomas Paine, Esq.'.[13]

Common Sense and the *Crisis* series were reprinted in England so that when Paine returned to that country in 1787, after 13 years in America, he was hailed as a great expounder of individual liberties. Among many he was known by his pen name 'Common Sense'. Paine visited Edmund Burke at Beaconsfield; he met with Charles James Fox, the Marquis of Lansdowne, Earl Fitzwilliam, Lord Stanhope and other prominent Whigs. He had no apparent political objectives on his trip to England. He had developed a plan for building an iron bridge of single span adequate to cross the Schuylkill River at Philadelphia. The Pennsylvania fathers were sceptical about such an ambitious programme, and on the advice of Ben Franklin, Paine took his models to England and France, hoping to get approvals from their scientific societies that would impress the American sceptics.

But Paine found that he was soon involved in politics once more, despite the purity of his original intentions. While in France he had resumed relations with Lafayette, whom he had known in America, and he became friendly with Condorcet and other leading French liberals. He was delighted, of course, with the first stirrings of the French Revolution, as were most of the liberals in England. Not delighted was Edmund Burke, who saw in the lawlessness of the taking of the Bastille in July 1789 a foretaste of increasing violence which might at length engulf England as well as France. In November 1790 Burke published his *Reflections on the Revolution in France*. Paine followed quickly with his *Rights of Man*. Professor Copeland wrote that 'The great controversy in which Burke and Paine were the principal antagonists was perhaps the most crucial ideological debate ever carried on in English.'[14] In this contest, Paine not only defended the French Revolution; he went out of his way to attack the English form of government: the monarchy was a tyranny, king and nobility were unnecessary. A convention should be called to establish a

5

republican government in England. In brief, England should have a revolution too. Paine gleefully wrote in February 1792 that revolution 'may be considered as the order of the day'.[15] Everybody should have one.

Paine's *Rights of Man* enjoyed enormous popularity in England,[16] though not with the government under the leadership of William Pitt. The government replied to Paine with a barrage of repressive measures. The King signed a proclamation against seditious measures, aimed specifically at Paine; a criminal action was brought against him for treason; and the administration hired an accomplished author, a man named George Chalmers, to write a scurrilous biography of Paine. Paine had never said much, at least in print, about his early years, and Chalmers' biography, published in July 1791, under the pseudonym 'Francis Oldys, A.M. of the University of Pennsylvania', told a story that removed Paine from the classification of gentleman, a position he had occupied by default for some years. Chalmers revealed that Paine, as a young man, had been a maker of corsets like his father; he had held ignominious jobs in the excise service which paid £50 a year and from which he had twice been fired; he had been a bankrupt; he had been twice married: the first wife died eleven months afterward, and the second marriage was never consummated, although Paine had lived with his second wife for three years.[17] Paine never answered these allegations, and except for occasional comments from his friends, the Chalmers life remained, and still remains today, the principal source of information about the first 37 years of Paine's life. The Paine biographer has been handed a host of questions: how much credence should Chalmers' allegations be given? For example, what can one say about the death of the first wife, which was caused, Chalmers claimed, by the maltreatment she received from her husband? And what about the second marriage that was never consummated? And had not Paine created the impression in America that he was a bachelor?

Investigations into Paine's early years run into a brick wall. Except for a formal letter to Oliver Goldsmith, there is not a single known letter either to or from Paine at any time in the entire first half of his life. Even Chalmers was unable to scrape up information for periods as long as five years at a time, leaving large gaps in the history.[18] There are similar gaps during the 13 years he was in America. He was engaged in seven projects or employments in that period. They account for a total of 48 months, or roughly a third of the time that he was in America.[19] We have only vague impressions on how he spent the remaining two-thirds of his time.

The Chalmers' life was reprinted in America in somewhat abbreviated form by William Cobbett. It became the source of most subsequent biographies of Paine, including the entry for Paine in the *Dictionary of National Biography*. It was not until Conway's biography was published in 1892 that any major effort was made to change the impression that Chalmers had created.

Larger questions emerge from the repressive measures of the Pitt administrations. Not only was Paine prosecuted and eventually outlawed as a traitor in England, but up until 1824 both publishers and vendors of the *Rights of Man* were fined and imprisoned;[20] the leaders of associations formed for the purpose of promoting parliamentary reform were prosecuted for distributing the *Rights of Man*; and the Habeas Corpus act was suspended in 1794 largely because of Paine's work. Was this because the establishment feared an uprising stimulated by Paine's writings, or were Paine's pamphlets used as a device by those in power to consolidate their position? Historians have taken both sides of this question.[21]

Shortly before he was scheduled to stand trial for treason, Paine went to France to serve as a member of the National Convention. At the outset he was regarded as the representative of America (which had no minister in Paris from 1789 to 1972). Lafayette even gave Paine the key to the Bastille to be delivered to George Washington.[22]

Paine had served in the National Convention for only four months when that body took up the question of what should be done with Louis XVI. The majority voted for the death penalty. Paine argued that the King should be spared, that he should be imprisoned for the duration of the war, and thereafter sent to America to live in exile.

Paine himself was in danger of the guillotine before the year was out. Once war was declared against England early in 1793, English citizens were arrested, Paine included, although he had been made an honorary French citizen. The American minister in Paris at that time was Gouverneur Morris, one of the many persons of influence that Paine had offended.[23] Morris did not like Paine any more than Paine liked Morris. Some 15 years earlier Morris had declared to Congress that Paine was 'a meer [sic] adventurer from England, without fortune, without family or connections, ignorant even of grammar, and who had lamely submitted to be kicked and cuffed from one end of America to the other'.[24]

The French authorities held Paine in gaol as an English subject. Paine claimed he was an American citizen, and Morris made an effort, but only a very perfunctory one, to gain Paine's freedom as an American. Thus Paine remained in prison from December 1793 to November 1794, throughout the Terror, when most of Paine's French friends were guillotined by Robespierre. What saved Paine was that Robespierre himself was guillotined in July 1794. Then Morris was succeeded as minister by James Monroe, who claimed Paine as an American citizen and obtained his release.

In Robespierre's papers, revealed after his death, was a note in his handwriting that Paine should be accused 'for the interests of America as much as of France'.[25] So it is clear that if Robespierre had lived, Paine would have followed the fate of his French friends. But what wonderful, puzzling questions: Why should Paine be accused for the interests of France? And much more interesting and more puzzling, why should Paine be accused for the interests of *America*? Was Gouverneur Morris the hatchetman? The paucity of Paine material in the Morris papers held by Columbia University invites the question of whether at some point the files were sanitized.

Paine's wrath at the nine months' imprisonment was, however, directed principally at the American president, the idol of his people, George Washington. Washington was an austere man, but he had displayed surprising warmth in his relations with Paine, inviting him on at least one occasion to 'partake of my Board' and assuring him that 'I shall be exceedingly happy to see you'.[26] According to Paine it was Washington's indifference to his fate that kept him in jail. Despite efforts made by Monroe to stop him, Paine sent for publication in America a long letter in which he alleged that Washington was 'treacherous in private friendship' and 'a hypocrite in public life', and that Washington would have been pleased to see Paine executed by the French.[27] Paine never applied his pen more viciously than against the first President of the United States.

What blame, the historian must ask, can properly be assigned to Washington? Morris appears to have sent two messages about Paine to America, both addressed to Jefferson as Secretary of State.[28] But Jefferson had resigned that post before either of the letters could have arrived, and he was succeeded by Edmund Randolph. The first message from Morris reported the imprisonment and suggested that Paine was safer in gaol, where he might be forgotten, than he would have been if his name had been brought to the attention of the French authorities who were busily sending their enemies to the guillotine. The second message stated that Morris had claimed Paine as an American citizen (although doing so was contrary to Morris's judgement), and that the claim had been denied. Randolph then notified Washington that Morris had demanded Paine's release as an American, but the French held Paine as one 'amenable to French laws'.[29]

Can we assume that Washington knew or should have suspected that Morris's application for Paine's release was made in bad faith? Can we conclude that it was within Washington's power to remedy the situation by a personal appeal to someone in the French government, having in mind that Washington's particular friend, Lafayette, was out of power and in an Austrian prison? Or was Paine's complaint based on the fact that, when Monroe was made minister, Washington had not asked him to 'look into' Paine's imprisonment? Almost certainly Monroe would have told Paine if Washington had made any such suggestion; on the other hand, Monroe's appointment antedated the receipt of Morris's first message about Paine, and Monroe's first report from Paris expressed surprise to find Paine in prison.[30] At a minimum, Paine could have argued, Washington should have sent some note of good cheer, even if only to congratulate him on his release.

During his imprisonment Paine had published the last of his great works: *The Age of Reason* — a frontal assault on the Christian religion and the authenticity of the Bible. The points raised by Paine were ones that scholars had been debating for hundreds of years. But Paine, for the first time, presented these doubts and arguments to the common man, creating a gigantic stir in both England and America.

Paine had grown disillusioned with the Revolution in France long before he was able to leave that country, even well before he was imprisoned; equally the French were disillusioned with him.[31] Paine's attack on Washington lost him friends in France where Washington was looked on as a god, and Washington's death in 1799 at age 67, increased, if anything, the reverence for him in Europe as well as in America. As long as England and France were at war, Paine (who had been found guilty of treason in England) could not risk capture by a British warship. Therefore it was not until the brief cessation of hostilities in 1802, following the Peace of Amiens, that Paine felt he could safely return to the United States.

When Paine finally got back to America in 1802 he quickly discovered that he was no longer a popular hero. He disembarked from his ship in Baltimore where the principal hotels refused to accept him. He found a place to stay in Washington only through the help of Thomas Jefferson.[32] Paine's attack on President Washington was not the only action held against him. There was also his attack on Christianity in *Age of Reason*.[33] Paine, who had left an America in 1787 that had large numbers of influential deists, returned 15 years later to an America engulfed in a religious revival for which Paine, to a large degree, was himself responsible.[34] The revulsion felt for Paine's *Age of Reason* and for other anti-religious thought was so great that a major counter-revolution had been set under way in America before the end of the eighteenth century. In 1796 every student at Harvard was given a copy of a book written by the English Bishop Watson entitled *An Apology for the Bible in a Series of Letters addressed to Thomas Paine*.[35] And the same thing was done at Yale. The anti-deist witch-hunt in America had gone so far that Joseph Willard, the president of Harvard, felt it necessary to announce that *The Decline and Fall of the Roman Empire* by Edward Gibbon was not used at Harvard![36]

When Paine discovered the strength of the religious revival in America, he attempted to justify his own position, but this brought him a rather sharp warning from his old friend Samuel Adams:

> When I heard that you had turned your mind to a defence of infidelity I felt myself much astonished, and more grieved, that you had attempted a measure so injurious to the feelings and so repugnant to the true interest of so great a part of the Citizens of the United States. The people of New England, if you will allow me to use a Scriptural phrase, are fast returning to their first love. Will you excite among them the Spirit of angry controversy at a time when they are hastening to Charity and Peace?[37]

Paine was not the sort of man to take advice from anyone. Years before, Benjamin Franklin had warned him to abandon his attacks on religion, but Paine thought he knew best.[38]

There was another change in America that affected Paine's reception there. During the time he was abroad the country had been split into two bitterly opposed parties: the conservatives, like John Adams, known as the Federalists (although confederation was no longer an issue), and the liberals, like Jefferson, known sometimes as the Democrats and sometimes as the Republicans.

Several months after his return to America, Paine wrote in a letter to a friend: 'America is not the same country as when I left it. This federal faction has debased its politics and corrupted its morality.'[39] The federal faction would have said — and did say — exactly the same thing of Paine with at least equal plausibility.

The admirers of Washington, the orthodox Christians and the Federalists did not permit Paine to lead the idyllic life in America he had so often dreamed of while in exile in France.[40] He was denied the right to vote in New Rochelle, New York, on the grounds that he was not an American citizen, and for supporting evidence was offered the reluctance of Gouverneur Morris to reclaim Paine in Paris. When Paine died in 1809 he was an unhappy and lonely man, his great days largely forgotten. The Quakers of New York denied his request to be buried in their graveyard, and he was interred on a corner of his farm at New Rochelle.

Paine's life as a whole raises one gigantic question:

11

'Explain, if you can', says a small voice to the biographer, 'how a man who had been such a resounding failure in England during the first 37 years of his life, could become almost overnight such a great success in America?' 'And why', continues the voice, 'was the success followed by such negative results — failures if you will — in England and France?' Finally, there is a third part to this question: 'why was the great patriot so widely rejected when he returned to America to end his days in peace?'

Notes

1. Benjamin Franklin to Richard Bache, 30 September 1774, quoted in Moncure Conway, *The Life of Thomas Paine* (New York: G.P. Putnam, 1892), vol. 1, p. 40; *The Writings of Benjamin Franklin* (New York: Macmillan, 1906), vol. VI, p. 248.

2. The Lee Papers, *Collections of the New York Historical Society* for 1871 (New York, 1872), vol. III, p. 119.

3. Page Smith, *John Adams* (New York: Doubleday, 1962), vol. I, p. 239.

4. Thomas Jefferson to Francis Epps, 19 January 1821, *The Family Letters of Thomas Jefferson*, eds Edwin M. Betts and James A. Bear (Columbia, Mo.: University of Missouri Press, 1966), p. 438.

5. *Crisis*, II (13 January 1775), in *The Complete Writings of Thomas Paine*, ed. Philip S. Foner (New York: The Citadel Press, 1945) (hereafter *Writings*), vol. I, p. 72; *Crisis* XIII (19 April 1783), in *Writings*, vol. I, p. 235. See also Letter IV 'To the Citizens of the United States' (3 December 1802), in *Writings*, vol. II, p. 926. John Adams remarked of an encounter with Paine that 'He was extremely earnest to convince me, that common [*sic*] Sense was his first born; declared again and again that he had never written a Line nor a Word that had been printed before Common Sense' (*Diary and Autobiography of John Adams* (New York: Belknap Press, 1961), vol. III, p. 334).

6. Ambrose Serle to Lord Dartmouth (Dartmouth Papers, vol. II, p. 439).

7. *Bulletin* of the Thomas Paine Society, vol. VI, no. 3 (1979), pp. 59-78.

8. Ibid., vol. VII, no. 2 (1982), pp. 53-5.

9. *Writings*, vol. I, pp. 4, 17, 45.

10. *Rights of Man*, pt. II, *Writings*, vol. I, p. 406.

11. Albert J. Beveridge, *The Life of John Marshall* (New York: Houghton Mifflin, 1916), vol. II, p. 12.

12. *Diary of a Common Soldier in the American Revolution, 1775-1783*, eds Robert C. Bray and Paul E. Bushnell (DeKalb, Illinois: Northern Illinois University Press, 1978), p. 266.

13. *Pennsylvania Journal*, 21 January 1786.

14. Thomas W. Copeland, *Our Eminent Friend, Edmund Burke* (1949) (Westport, Conn: Greenwood, 1970), p. 148.

15. *Rights of Man*, pt. II, *Writings*, vol. I, p. 355.

16. Philip Foner claims that close to a million and a half copies were sold during Paine's lifetime (*Writings*, vol. I, p. 345).

17. Other uncomplimentary comments were added with the passage of time. See, for example, *Gentleman's Magazine* (1803), pp. 332-3. The claim here is that Paine was born out of wedlock.

18. The five-year blank was from 1752 to 1757 when Paine was 15 to 20 years of age.

19. Editor of *Pennsylvania Magazine*, six months; secretary to Pennsylvania volunteers, three months; aide to General Green, three months; secretary to Congressional Committee, nine months; clerk to Owen Biddle, seven months; clerk to Pennsylvania Assembly, twelve months; in Paris with John Laurens, eight months.

20. Joel H. Wiener, *Radicalism and Freethought in Nineteenth-century Britain: The Life of Richard Carlile* (Westport, Conn.: Greenwood, 1983), p. 96.

21. For the less common view that Paine's writing was used as a device to consolidate power, see William T. Latrobe, 'England and the French Revolution 1789-1797', *Johns Hopkins Studies in Historical and Political Science*, vol. XXVII, nos 8-12 (August-December 1909).

22. Paine to George Washington, 1 May 1790, *Writings*, vol. II, p. 1302.

23. In his letter to Secretary of State Thomas Jefferson, dated 13 February 1792, Paine stated that the Morris appointment was 'a most unfortunate one and as I shall mention the same thing to him when I see him, I do not express it to you with the injunction of a confidence' (*Writings*, vol. II, p. 1323).

24. Gouverneur Morris Papers (Columbia University).

25. Conway, *Paine*, vol. II, p. 81.

26. Washington to Paine, 10 September 1783, *The Writings of George Washington* (Washington: US Government Printing Office, 1938), vol. XXVII, p. 146.

27. Paine to George Washington, 30 July 1796, *Writings*, vol. II, p. 691. James Monroe to Madison, 5 July 1796: 'Paine ... thinks the President winked at his imprisonment and wishes he might die in gaol', *The Writings of James Monroe* (New York: G.P. Putnam's Sons, 1900), vol. II, p. 20.

28. Gouverneur Morris to Thomas Jefferson, 21 January 1794, 6 March 1794, *The Life and Correspondence of Gouverneur Morris* (Boston: Gray and Bowen, 1832), vol. II, pp. 393, 408. Jefferson resigned on 31 December 1793 (Dumas Malone, *Jefferson and The Ordeal of Liberty* (Boston: Little, Brown & Co., 1962), vol. III, p. 161).

29. Edmund Randolph to George Washington, 25 July 1794 (Conway, *Paine*, vol. II, p. 125).

30. Monroe was appointed minister to France in May 1794. This was the month before Randolph informed Washington of Paine's imprisonment. (Monroe to Randolph, 7 November 1794: 'I was extremely concerned, upon my arrival here, to find our countryman, Mr. Paine, and likewise Madame Lafayette were in prison ... I assured them ... of the regard entertained for them by the President', *Writings of James Monroe*, vol. II (1899), p. 106.) In a letter to Paine, Monroe wrote of Washington's 'friendly dispositions

towards you ... I forward his wishes in seeking your safety' (Monroe to Paine, 18 September 1794), *Writings of James Monroe*, vol. VII (1903), pp. 296-7.

31. Paine to Jefferson, 20 April 1793, *Writings*, vol. II, p. 1331; Malone, *Jefferson*, vol. III, p. 186. See *Le Republicaine Français*, 30 December 1796.

32. Dumas Malone, *Jefferson the President* (Boston: Little, Brown & Co., 1970), vol. IV, pp. 195-9; J.W. Knudsen, 'The Rage Around Tom Paine', *New York Historical Society Quarterly*, vol. LIII (January 1969), pp. 60-1.

33. Paine's criticism of the American constitution of 1789 ('it ought to be kicked out') was another cause of his unpopularity.

34. A 'Thomas Paine' of Boston in 1803 announced that he was changing his name to 'a Christian one', thereafter being known as Robert Treat Paine, Jr. (Knudsen, 'Tom Paine', p. 60).

35. *Memoirs of Daniel Appleton White*, ed. James Walker (Massachusetts Historical Society, 1863), vol. VI, p. 267; *Memoirs of William Ellery Channing* (Boston, 1840), vol. I, p. 61.

36. *Columbian Centinel*, 16 November 1791.

37. Samuel Adams to Paine, 30 November 1802, *The Writings of Samuel Adams* (New York: G.P. Putnam, 1908), vol. IV, pp. 412-13.

38. See Franklin to Ezra Stiles, 9 March 1790, *The Writings of Benjamin Franklin* (New York: Macmillan, 1907), vol. X, p. 85.

39. Paine to Elisha Babcock, 10 October 1803. The Spater Papers do not contain reference to the location of this letter.

40. The Federalist newspapers referred to Paine as an 'obscene old sinner', 'the living opprobrium of humanity', 'an infamous scavenger'. *The Columbian Centinel*, a strong supporter of Paine during the Paine–Burke debate of 1791-2, had become a bitter detractor by 1801, calling Paine a 'drunkard' and a 'buffoon'.

PART ONE

1 The Early Years, 1737-74

George Spater

On 29 January 1737, Thomas Paine was born at Thetford, in the County of Norfolk, to Joseph and Frances Paine, a hard-working couple who lived in conditions of respectable poverty. Joseph Paine, a stay-maker of Quaker background, was tolerant and easy-going; by contrast his wife, Frances, eleven years older than her husband, was Anglican by faith, severe and repressive by temperament. The couple had been married by an Anglican priest. Besides Thomas they had one other child, Elizabeth, who was born on 29 August 1738.[1]

Thomas's relations with his father were affectionate while with his mother they were, at best, dutiful. These facts can be inferred from his references to his parents in his subsequent writings. They are important for an understanding of his development; for though almost certainly baptised according to Anglican rites, like his sister Elizabeth, and quite certainly confirmed in the Anglican Church, Thomas retained 'much of the Quaker in both temperament and ideas'.[2] As Dr Henry Collins put it,

His writing, while powerful and often illuminated by flashes of vehemence or wit, was free from the self-conscious polish and formal rhetoric which featured so strongly in eighteenth-century English prose. Apart from the Quaker plainness in his style of writing and of life, Quaker values had a lasting influence on his ideas. His

17

implicit assumptions were egalitarian. All men were created equal since they were equally the children of God.[3]

It is impossible to say at what stage in his life Paine became freethinking and exposed to the influence of the humanitarian aspects of the Enlightenment, but according to later recollections it began very early indeed. When he was seven or eight, after hearing a sermon from a member of his family on the crucifixion, he 'went into the garden, and as I was going down the garden steps (for I perfectly remember the spot), I revolted at the recollection of what I had heard, and thought to myself that it was making God Almighty act like a passionate man who killed His son when He could not revenge himself in any other way; and, as I was sure a man would be hanged who did such a thing, I could not see for what purpose they preached such sermons.'[4]

Nevertheless, though Quakerism was present in his background from the beginning, and was, throughout, to permeate his attitudes and values, Paine's religious background was Anglican, and it would be half a century before he would break with organised religion. Meanwhile, other influences were present which were to lead him, much earlier, into collision with authority.

Among these early influences must be counted Paine's brief encounter with formal education. Some of the boys at Thetford Grammar School were taught Latin but Paine was not among them. Latin, 'in the society of eighteenth-century England', as Henry Collins observed, 'was the normal passport into the world of letters, and this fact, too, was to leave its mark on Paine throughout his life. His later reading, though wide, was patchy, and his cast of mind was never academic.'[5] On balance this was to turn out a considerable advantage to a man of his peculiar temperament. He learned enough, at school, to be able to express himself in his own words, and it was through his genius in this respect that he became a force in popular history. As he would later say, 'I scarcely ever quote; the reason is, I always think.'[6]

Having left school in 1750, Paine followed the not uncommon course of working with his father, learning to make corsets. For a child of poor parents it was essential, wherever possible, to learn a skilled trade; the alternative would be, at best, a life of casual labour interspersed with periods of unemployment, a path which led, all too often, to the work-house and a pauper's grave. Paine stayed with his father until 1754. We cannot be sure how he spent the next three years, which may have included a spell at sea, but by 1757, at the age of 20, Paine was working as a stay-maker in the shop of a Mr Morris in London. 'The natural bent of my mind,' he wrote later in reference to his schooldays, 'was to science', and for Paine a domicile in London would present the first opportunity for following up his scientific interests. 'As soon as I was able', he continued, 'I purchased a pair of globes, and attended the philosophical lectures of Martin and Ferguson, and became afterward acquainted with Dr. Bevis, of the society called the Royal Society, then living in the Temple, and an excellent astronomer.' 'I had no disposition', Paine was careful to add, 'for what is called politics. It presented to my mind no other idea than as contained in the word Jockey-ship'.[7]

It was to be some years before Paine was to view politics as anything other than a matter of jockeying for position between rival groups, the fortunes and misfortunes of which could have no bearing on anything in which he was inter-ested. For anyone in his position the prime concern would be to keep alive in tolerable conditions; hence time was of the essence for the 20-year-old Paine to set himself up in business as a craftsman. After a brief period in London he moved to Dover, and in April 1759, he opened his own shop as a master stay-maker in Sandwich. Five months later, in September, he married an orphan, Mary Lambert, and the couple set up house on Dolphin Key.[8] It was one of the very few periods of ordinary domestic life that Paine was to know. Business was bad, and the young couple moved to Margate. Shortly after-wards his wife died and Paine decided to abandon his trade. His wife's father had once been a customs officer, and after seeking the advice of his own father, who responded favour-ably, Paine spent a few months studying the profession in London before returning to Thetford in July 1761. In 1762 he was appointed to examine brewers' casks at Grantham, Lincolnshire, and in 1763 he was moved to Alford, nearer the coast, and, at the time, a favourite centre for smugglers. Public sympathy was, for obvious reasons, on the side of the smugglers, and excisemen were, as a profession, unpopular. They were also poorly paid, and in consequence, corrupt; most of them, including Paine, performed their duties in a perfunctory manner. Consignments were sometimes stamped without being properly inspected or even, on occasions, visited. For some such lapse Paine was discharged in August 1765.[9]

After returning to work as a journeyman stay-maker, Paine moved back to London where he found work as a school-master, teaching English for a Mr Noble in Goodman's Fields, and soon afterwards for a Mr Gardiner at Kensington. According to a contemporary account,[10] Paine, who was fond of preaching, wished at the time to enter the Church, but was prevented from doing so by his ignorance of Latin. As a schoolmaster he was earning even less than as a customs officer, and he soon formally applied for reinstatement in the excise service. Since the sort of casualness for which he had been discharged was extremely common at prevailing salaries, he was readily re-employed.

In February 1768, Paine resumed work as an exciseman, this time at Lewes, in Sussex, where he was to remain until his departure for America nearly seven years later. He lodged with Samuel Ollive, a tobacconist, in Lewes High Street.[11] Ollive had been active in the local government of the borough since 1745, and he remained so up to his death in July 1769. During the period of over a year in which they had been together, it seems that Samuel Ollive introduced Paine to local politics, because a few weeks after his landlord's death, Paine was elected a member of the Lewes Town Council, then known as the Council of Twelve.[12] While continuing to work as an exciseman, Paine helped Samuel Ollive's widow to run her tobacconist's shop, and on 26 March 1771, at the age of 34, he married the Ollives' daughter, Elizabeth.

For the first time in his life Paine was now actively engaged in public life. He remained a member of the Council of Twelve until October 1772, after which he became absorbed in a national campaign by excisemen to improve their appalling conditions. By this time Paine was a well-known figure in Lewes through his activities on the Council; he was also renowned as a vociferous and well-liked member of the Headstrong Club — a discussion and social club which met in the White Hart, not far from the Ollive's premises in the High Street. Considering himself a Whig, his views at the time appear to have been liberal rather than radical, and certainly in no way subversive. However, his personal affairs were not thriving and he was proving no more successful as part-manager of a tobacconist's than he had previously been as a master stay-maker. The business was not flourishing when Samuel Ollive died. Paine's assistance to Ollive's widow did little to improve matters. Meanwhile, he took the initiative in organising a petition among his fellow excisemen for an improvement in their rates of pay. He collected three shillings a head from his colleagues throughout the country and drafted a petition backed by a pamphlet of which 4,000 copies were printed.

This pamphlet, *The Case of the Officers of the Excise*, was Paine's first known work, though it was not issued for sale to the public until 1793, by which time its author had achieved international fame. *The Case of the Officers* is not a political statement, but it does contain ideas which were to appear, considerably elaborated, in his later writings. The core of his argument was that existing salaries were too low to attract the quality of recruits required by excise work, and that it was unwise, to say the least, to under-pay officers in a service which was so prone to corruption. But, in addition, there were two further arguments: one overtly economic, the other by implication political. For the first time Paine put on record his views about inflation, which he was later to develop in more detail. Paine drew attention to 'the high price of provisions' which he attributed directly to 'the increase of money in the kingdom'. Rising prices might bring 'affluence' to some, while others might find their market position strong enough to enable them to increase the price of their goods and services so as at least to offset the effect of rising costs. For instance, 'the mechanic and the labourer may in a great measure ward off the distress by raising the price of their manufactures or their work, but the situation of the officers admits of no such relief'. Paine's other main point contained political implications which he did not make explicitly and which he might or might not have realised. For example he suggested that the dangers of corruption might be under-estimated by those who had not experienced poverty at first hand. Nearly 20 years later, in Part I of the *Rights of Man*, Paine was to draw political conclusions from the fact that the rich and privileged lived in ignorance of the material conditions in which the majority of their countrymen lived. But, in *The Case of the Officers of the Excise*, Paine was drafting a humble petition rather than an ardent demand for human rights. The excisemen had no bargaining power, nor even a permanent organisation, but Paine was convinced that 'There are some cases so singularly reasonable, that the more they are considered, the more weight they obtain'.[13] This idea, too, with its assertion of faith in the power of human reason, was to recur in Paine's writings, though in radically altered form.

Paine's efforts on behalf of the excisemen were without effect, except to expedite his own discharge from the service, and to bring him into contact with men who were to influence decisively the future course of his life. During the winter of 1772-3 he spent a good deal of time in London, lobbying members of Parliament and trying to enlist support from the eminent in other walks of life. This brought him into contact with the writer Oliver Goldsmith and, more particularly, with Benjamin Franklin, a Bostonian, one of the leading representatives of the American colonists in London, who had been actively concerned in the tortuous and rapidly deteriorating relations between the English government and the North American colonists. While soliciting support for the excisemen, Paine met Franklin, with whom he shared a strong interest in science, and who was clearly impressed by him. Paine's prolonged absences in London, in 1773-4, must have contributed to the failure of the tobacconist's business in Lewes, as well as to Paine's estrangement from his wife. The second quarter of 1774 was a black period in Paine's life. On 8 April he was dismissed, finally, from the excise; six days later his business was sold, and on 4 June he finally separated from his wife.[14]

In October of the same year Paine left for America with a letter of introduction from Benjamin Franklin to his son-in-law, Richard Bache, in which Franklin described Paine as 'an ingenious worthy young man. He goes to Pennsylvania with a view of settling there ... If you can put him in a way of obtaining employment as a clerk, or assistant tutor in a school, or assistant surveyor ... so that he may procure a subsistence at least, [you will] ... much oblige your affectionate father.'[15] With these modest expectations, and after almost dying from typhus on the voyage, Paine was carried ashore at Philadelphia on 30 November to start a new and spectacular chapter in his hitherto unpromising life.

Notes

1. See Alfred O. Aldridge, *Man of Reason: The Life of Thomas Paine* (New York: J.B. Lippincott, 1959), pp. 13-14. Horne Tooke was a leading radical who had actively supported John Wilkes during the 1760s. He was later a member of the Society for Promoting Constitutional Information which promoted the sale of *Rights of Man* during the 1790s.

2. Henry Collins, 'Introduction', in *Rights of Man* (1791-2) (Harmondsworth: Penguin, 1969), p. 11.

3. Ibid., p. 11.

4. *The Age of Reason* (1794), *Writings*, vol. I, p. 497.

5. Collins, 'Introduction', p. 11.

6. 'The Forester's Letters', no. III (1776), in *Writings*, vol. II, p. 78.

7. *Age of Reason*, *Writings*, vol. I, p. 496. On Paine's innovative use of language, see Olivia Smith, *The Politics of Language* (Oxford: Clarendon Press, 1984), esp. ch. II.

8. Conway, *Paine*, vol. I, p. 15.

9. Ibid., pp. 16-18; Aldridge, *Man of Reason*, p. 16.

10. By George Chalmers (pseud. Francis Oldys), who wrote a scurrilous 'biography' of Paine in 1791.

11. This is now the Bull House, High Street, Lewes.

12. See Collins, 'Introduction', p. 13n.

13. *The Case of the Officers of the Excise* (1772), *Writings*, vol. II, pp. 13-15.

14. David Freeman Hawke, *Paine* (New York: Harper & Row, 1974), p. 19.

15. Conway, *Paine*, vol. I, p. 16.

2 American Revolutionary, 1774-89

George Spater

We cannot be sure about the nature of the political ideas entertained by Paine upon his arrival in America. Since the early 1760s, England had experienced a ferment of democratic activity, most notably in the form of the popular cry of 'Wilkes and Liberty'. Doubtless this ferment was represented in the debates at the White Hart in Lewes, where Paine, according to his friend Thomas 'Clio' Rickman, was in politics a Whig, 'and notorious for that quality which has been defined perseverance in a good cause and obstinacy in a bad one. He was tenacious of his opinions, which were bold, acute, and independent, and which he maintained with ardour, elegance, and argument.'[1] In political theory the background to the debates would have been the works of John Locke, but according to Paine's account, written towards the end of his life, 'I never read Locke ... and by what I have heard of it from *Horne Tooke*, I had no inducement to read it. It is a speculative, not a practical work, and the style of it is heavy and tedious.'[2] Nevertheless, Locke, as Henry Collins remarked, 'influenced Paine at second hand'.[3] It is possible, too, that during Paine's meetings with Franklin in London, the latter might well have mentioned England's relations with her American colonies, which had, by 1774, reached an explosive state. However, there is no evidence for such a discussion; most of their talk probably reflected their mutual interest in engineering and science.

Franklin's letter of introduction secured Paine a warm welcome in Philadelphia, and he easily found employment as a tutor to the sons of a number of wealthy families. He soon acquired a considerable reputation and in his first letter to Franklin from America, on 4 March 1775, he described his early months in Philadelphia. Significantly, the letter refers to the 'experiments on air' of Dr Joseph Priestley, who was, like Franklin, one of the leading scientists of his day and who like Paine, was later to suffer persecution in England for his support of the French Revolution. Paine also told Franklin that he had met 'a Printer and Bookseller ... a man of reputation and property, a Robert Aitken' who had recently started *The Pennsylvania Magazine: or, American Monthly Record*.[4] Paine contributed an article to the first number, which appeared on 24 January 1775, in which he dealt with the role of the press in forming the culture of a new society.[5] It was not long before Paine was appointed editor, and by March the number of subscribers had more than doubled from the original figure of under 600. Circulation continued to grow rapidly.[6]

Paine's journalism was not confined to *The Pennsylvania Magazine*. On 8 March 1775, the *Pennsylvania Journal* published an article by him on 'African Slavery in America' which he signed with the *nom-de-plume*, 'Justice and Humanity'. Paine was by no means the first American to advocate the abolition of slavery. In 1769, Thomas Jefferson, who was later to become a close friend of Paine's and to serve as third President of the United States, had urged emancipation on the Assembly in Virginia, and there had been others before him. Nevertheless, Paine was among the first abolitionists. He argued that the institution of slavery was a violation of the 'natural' right to freedom of people who had committed no crime. He was also concerned with the fate of the freed slaves. Merely to turn them loose would be inadequate and, in many circumstances, cruel. Freed slaves who were elderly must be provided with pensions; and those who were young required land — either rented from their former masters or on America's expanding frontiers, where they could form 'useful barrier settlements'. Paine pointed to the incongruity of complaints by the colonists against England's trade in slaves while they tolerated, in their own country, an institution which was contrary at once to the 'light of nature' and the teachings of the 'Redeemer'.[7] On 14 April, a month after the article appeared, America's first anti-slavery society was formed, in Philadelphia, with Paine among its members. Also in the society was Dr Benjamin Rush, one of the pioneers of the Enlightenment in America who, a few months later, encouraged Paine to write his pamphlet *Common Sense* in support of American independence.

As far as we can tell, Paine as yet had no thoughts about American independence; certainly he published nothing on Anglo–American relations until after the fighting had broken out at Lexington and Concord on 19 April 1775. After this, his attacks on England became bitter and sustained, and it was not long before he was openly advocating independence at a time when only a tiny minority of Americans were thinking of anything beyond securing fairer treatment under the English Crown. In 'A Serious Thought', which appeared in the *Pennsylvania Journal* on 18 October, he indicted England for her barbarous cruelty towards Indians and Negro slaves. 'When I reflect finally on these', he declared, 'I hesitate not for a moment to believe that the Almighty will finally separate America from Britain. Call it independence or what you will.'[8] His sentiments were still cautiously expressed, but a revolutionary was in the making.

By beginning to advocate independence as the solution to America's problems, Paine was suddenly on the radical wing of American politics. On religious matters his development was more cautious. In his attack on slavery he used arguments drawn from the New Testament. His views were, in most respects, orthodox Christian, though undenominational; and while he occasionally described himself, or allowed himself to be described, as a 'Quaker' in a rather loose and general sense, he was never a member of a Quaker connection. By 1775 he may already have begun to wonder how far his Quaker-based humanitarianism was compatible with orthodox Christianity, although the only expression of such doubts, if he felt them, occurred in an article against the practice of duelling, which he denounced as an absurd survival of 'gothic' or medieval military values. He ended by commenting mildly on 'the peculiar prevalence of this custom in countries where the religious system is established'.[9]

Meanwhile, Paine had to come to terms with his Quaker-ism in a more directly political sense. While independence was not yet an issue, Americans were debating among themselves how far they were justified in taking up arms against their lawful sovereign. From his discussions in the White Hart, Paine had already absorbed the Whig version of popular sovereignty. He had written, as early as 4 January 1775, that 'A Briton or an American ceases to be a British subject when he ceases to be governed by rulers chosen or approved of by himself', though he had ended his article with a plea for a restoration of 'perpetual harmony between Britain and her colonies'.[10] Once fighting had broken out, however, Paine soon made clear that, whatever other attitudes he may have taken from the Quakers, he did not share their attitude to war. War was, of course, an evil, but it might in some conditions be necessary. In 'Thoughts on Defensive War', which he contributed to the *Pennsylvania Magazine* for July 1775, he wrote, 'I am thus far a Quaker, that I would gladly agree with all the world to lay aside the use of arms, and settle matters by negotiation; but unless the whole world will, the matter ends, and I take up my musket.' Paine presented his readers with the common-place reply to pacifism when he wrote that, if peace-lovers become pacifists, 'the peaceable part of mankind will be continually overrun by the vile and abandoned, while they neglect the means of self defence'.[11]

Throughout 1775 American politics were dominated by the confusion of an undeclared revolution. The Continental Congress, representing the Assemblies of the 13 dissident colonies, had met in Philadelphia in September of the previous year. By April 1775, it had become an unconstitutional body directing armed operations against the forces of the English sovereign. Yet, although such radical Englishmen as John Cartwright had been openly advocating American independence for more than a year, there was hardly an American colonist who was prepared for what seemed to most to be a desperate leap in the dark. In 1774, John Adams, who was to become President of the United States upon Washington's resignation in 1797, identified independence as 'a Hobgoblin of so frightful Mien, that it would throw a delicate Person into fits to look it in the Face'.[12] And by the end of 1775 it still seemed to most Americans who had supported the taking up of arms that they were fighting to restore the sovereign to his senses rather than to depose him and establish a republic. The small minority, however, which had been actively working for independence since the latter part of 1775, included two of Paine's friends in Philadelphia, Benjamin Franklin and Benjamin Rush, as well as Generals George Washington, Nathaniel Greene and Charles Lee in Cambridge, Massachusetts. To Thomas Paine, however, belongs the honour of being the first American to publish a call for independence; it came in the form of his pamphlet *Common Sense*, which appeared in Philadelphia on 10 January 1776.

We do not know how much of the pamphlet's contents were owed to Paine's discussions with Franklin and Rush, although we do know that when the pamphlet appeared anonymously, it was widely attributed to Franklin, and that while Paine was composing it he read it to Rush in instalments. However, we can be quite certain that the ideas expressed in *Common Sense* developed naturally from Paine's previous thinking and background, and that the style in which it was written was uniquely his. The work contained an attack on hereditary monarchy as an institution and on the exploitation of the poor by the rich which, in Paine's view, was facilitated by a monarchical regime. Paine was shrewd enough, as Henry Collins pointed out, to predict that monarchist France, in accordance with her national interests, would assist republican America, 'since both shared a common antagonism to England'.[13] It is significant that *Common Sense* appeared in French translation in May 1776, with the anti-monarchist passages deleted.

In America the success of Paine's pamphlet was immediate and spectacular. It sold well over 100,000 copies; and the author, characteristically, sacrificed the entire profits to the war effort.[14] According to Benjamin Rush, most citizens of Philadelphia were opposed to independence before *Common Sense* appeared,[15] and there is every reason to suppose that in this respect the chief city in Pennsylvania, which was to become the first capital of the United States, was typical. The effect of Paine's pamphlet was almost instantaneous. By 14 February 1776, it was in its third edition, and by the end of March, George Washington was writing to Colonel Reed: 'I find that "Common Sense" is working a powerful change here in the minds of many men.'[16]

Paine was now launched on a career of political writing which was to last for the next 30 years. The influence of *Common Sense* was not confined to North America. We have already referred to the appearance of a French translation within four months of the original, and Silas Deane, the colonists' chief representative in France, with whom Paine's future relations were to be so bitter, was to report in August that the French edition had probably sold more copies than the original. Some 13 years later a Spanish translation was to appear, and soon there was another Spanish translation in Central and South America, where it was to exert a powerful influence on the independence movements which destroyed the Spanish Empire.[17]

Meanwhile, on 28 June 1776, the Continental Congress elected a committee of five to draft the Declaration of Independence. The historic document, which appeared on 4 July, though written by Jefferson, was to convey, in Henry Collins' words, 'the indelible imprint of *Common Sense*'.[18] Jefferson was one of the few American politicians who remembered this, and he was to remain loyal to Paine — often at some political cost — through all the controversies which were to figure so prominently throughout the whole of Paine's political life.

From its first appearance, *Common Sense* became a centre of controversy. To the Tories and to conservatively-minded Whigs, who were numerous in 'respectable' Philadelphia, Paine's doctrine of 'Independence and Republicanism' was unacceptable. Beginning in April a series of letters appeared in the *Pennsylvania Gazette* attacking Paine's pamphlet. Signed 'Cato', they were written by the Rev. Dr William Smith, one of the colony's leading Anglican clergymen.[19] Paine replied immediately in the columns of the *Pennsylvania Journal* in a series known as 'The Forester's Letters'. For a writer who has so frequently been regarded as a shallow demagogue, ignorant of the world and arguing *a priori* from unsound philosophical premises, Paine showed a degree of political judgement and acumen which was, for a man of his admittedly limited experience, almost uncanny. He claimed, for example, that relations between Britain and the colonists had reached the point of no return. There were no terms on which agreement could be reached since 'If they be calculated to please the Cabinet they will not go down with the colonies: and if they be suited to the colonies they will be rejected by the Cabinet.' By April 1776, this was almost certainly true; moreover it was precisely the kind of argument which was most likely to affect the minds of the still numerous waverers who were plainly scared of the dangerous revolutionary course on which America had embarked, and who had not yet abandoned hopes of reconciliation with the home government. In fact, argued Paine, such fears were exaggerated, since America would not lack allies, and he predicted, accurately enough, that foreign aid would be forthcoming from European powers wishing to 'partake of a free and uninterrupted trade with the whole Continent of America'. This gave Smith the opportunity of charging Paine with wanting to bring in the armies of foreign governments to settle American affairs. Paine dealt easily with this by retorting that, since the colonists did not lack numbers, 'The assistance which we hope for from France is not armies (we want them not) but arms and ammunition', which had, indeed, already started to arrive. Anticipating a doctrine he was later to elaborate in the *Rights of Man*, Paine denied, in the third of 'The Forester's Letters', that any government could claim a *right* to rule by reason of legitimacy, or, indeed, by any criterion except popular consent and the people's interests. 'Government', he maintained, 'should always be considered as a matter of convenience, not of right.' Finally, with extraordinary perceptiveness, Paine challenged, in the fourth Letter, the widely accepted view, which Smith had repeated, that popular government would necessarily be hostile to property. On the contrary, Paine asserted, under a popular government 'All property is safe' because 'division of property never entered the mind of the populace' — a view which was true, and which remained true throughout the eighteenth century and beyond.[20]

In August 1776, Paine joined the revolutionary army, and in September he became *aide-de-camp* to General Greene at Fort Lee, with the rank of brigade major. He was already a national figure, and as a result of the enormous circulation of *Common Sense*, 'The Forester's Letters' had also been widely reprinted. But, while political opinion was swinging in favour of independence and republicanism, the military position was gloomy, especially after the long retreat of General Washington and his forces from the Hudson and the Delaware towards Philadelphia. Congress abandoned the capital city for Baltimore; the situation seemed hopeless. On 19 December, Paine, who had gone to Philadelphia with the intention of allaying the panic, published the first of his *Crisis* papers in the *Pennsylvania Journal*. 'These are the times that try men's souls', he wrote in his opening line, responding exactly to the mood of the moment. 'The summer soldier and the sunshine patriot will, in this crisis, shrink from the service of his country; but he that stands it *now*, deserves the love and thanks of man and woman.'[21] This was to be the first of the sixteen *Crisis* papers, all of them appearing at critical points in the course of the Revolutionary War, until the final number, on 9 December 1783, after independence had been secured, pointed to the need for political unity among the 13 colonies, if the fruits of victory were not to be dissipated.

As he proceeded with the *Crisis* papers, Paine was elected by the Continental Congress as Secretary to its Committee of Foreign Affairs, in which capacity he played a leading part in the negotiations which were to culminate in the formal alliance with France in the following year. This new experience of political responsibility brought out some of the weakness, as well as the strength, of Paine's personal character. Reacting, as he did, to political events with extraordinary sensitivity and insight, he often displayed a very different side of his nature in the conduct of his personal affairs. And, where political and personal issues coincided, the results were sometimes disastrous. America was represented in France by two Commissioners, Arthur Lee and the plausible but shifty Silas Deane, a delegate to Congress from Connecticut. The French government, which had been defeated by England in the Seven Years' War in 1763, and suffered grievous colonial losses as a result, was very ready to help the American revolutionaries, and had been doing so on a significant scale since 1776. However, before the formal conclusion of the Franco–American alliance in 1778, it was important that such aid be kept secret, since it was contrary to diplomatic protocol between countries nominally at peace. When Deane returned to America in 1778 there were grounds for suspicion that he had used his part in the negotiations to line his own pockets. Paine was soon convinced that the suspicion was well founded, and he did not hesitate to say so in his usual forthright style.

Deane had influential friends, however, while Paine had important enemies. This may seem strange in view of his tremendous services to the American cause. Even James Cheetham, who quarrelled bitterly with Paine in the last years of his life, wrote in his posthumous and largely scurrilous biography, that the first of the *Crisis* papers was 'read in the camp, to every corporal's guard, and in the army and out of it had more than the intended effect. The convention of New York, reduced by dispersion, occasioned by alarm, to nine members, was rallied and reanimated. Militiamen who, already tired of the war, were straggling from the army, returned. Hope succeeded to despair, cheerfulness to gloom, and firmness to irresolution.'[22] Immediately afterwards, however, Paine had become involved in the controversy surrounding the new Constitution of Pennsylvania; his controversial stance was to defend the democratic side against those opposed to the idea of a single-chamber assembly. In doing so, in 1777, he made enemies among the more prosperous citizens, including aristocrats and wealthy merchants, who were afraid of what they considered to be the excessively democratic features of the Constitution. They included the financier Robert Morris and Gouverneur Morris, who was later, to Paine's cost, to serve as United States Ambassador to France. When in 1778, Silas Deane returned from France, he was accused by his fellow Commissioner, Lee, with having charged Congress for stores supplied by France as a gift. In the ensuing controversy, Paine bluntly declared in an article in the *Pennsylvania Packet* that the supplies for which Deane was demanding reimbursement from an impoverished Congress 'were promised and engaged, and ... as a present, before he ever *arrived* in France'.[23] This, while no doubt true, was highly embarrassing both to Congress and to the government of France. Congress repudiated Paine's statement and he was forced to resign as Secretary to the Committee on Foreign Affairs. Though Paine's statement was true enough, he had only been able to make it by using confidential documents which he had seen in his official capacity. History has vindicated Paine. Silas Deane later defected to Britain; his French partner, with whom he had cooked up the affair, was Caron de Beaumarchais. Like Silas Deane, the author of *The Barber of Seville* and *The Marriage of Figaro* was financially disreputable, even by eighteenth-century standards. Paine's conduct, on the other hand, was politically indefensible. He resigned with dignity but with a display of righteous indignation which could only have arisen from hypocrisy, or from a dangerous degree of unworldliness which he was to display too often in the future.[24]

Fortunately for Paine his party was victorious in the fight over the Constitution of Pennsylvania; hence he was not out of public affairs for long. In 1779 he was appointed Clerk to the Pennsylvania Assembly. Opinion in the Pennsylvania Assembly was hostile to slavery and Paine personally drafted the Preamble to an Act providing for the gradual abolition of slavery in the State — the first such Act in the history of the United States. The two other main issues which preoccupied Paine at the time were those of federal unity and war finance. On both he was to make a major contribution to the future of his adopted country.[25]

As a loose confederation of 13 independent colonies it was impossible to fight a successful war. General Washington, though Commander-in-Chief, had no authority over the forces voluntarily contributed by the separate colonies. Related to this was the issue of finance. When fighting broke out Congress had no power to levy taxes and was entirely dependent on such sums as the independent colonies chose to contribute. Morale among the troops, who were all too frequently both defeated and unpaid, was low, and as Paine was among the first to see, morale would be the decisive factor in determining the issue of the war. As early as 13 January 1777, in the second of his *Crisis* papers, he had informed Lord Howe, brother of the English Commander-in-Chief, who had arrived from England with an offer of free pardon for all rebels who surrendered, that 'The "UNITED STATES OF AMERICA", will sound as pompously in the world or in history, as "the kingdom of Great Britain"'.[26] Paine was probably the first person in the world to employ the term 'United States of America',[27] and it was consistently his policy_ to urge the colonies to sink their individual claims and interests in the common cause.

However, pending the creation of an effective system of war finance, emergency measures were essential, and Paine was one of the pioneers of the Bank of Pennsylvania which was later to become the Bank of North America. By the beginning of 1780, when Paine was to take his next initiative, the American cause looked desperate. The whole of Georgia was in British hands, and on 12 May 1780, General Lincoln was to surrender Charleston, South Carolina, together with his entire army of 5,000 men.[28] As Clerk to the Pennsylvania Assembly, Paine read, in closed session, a letter from George Washington couched in the gloomiest terms. 'I assure you', the General wrote, 'every idea you can form of our distresses will fall short of the reality. There is such a combination of circumstances to exhaust the patience of the soldiery that it begins at length to be worn out, and we see in every line of the army the most serious features of mutiny and sedition.' In view of this it was scarcely surprising that one member remarked that it was 'vain to contend the matter any longer. We may as well give up at first as at last'.[29]

Paine saw finance as the key to the situation. The machinery for collecting taxes was rudimentary and the government's credit non-existent. Paine characteristically donated 500 dollars to launch a fund which he suggested should provide the nucleus for a new Bank of Pennsylvania. This would provide the government with credit against the security of its post-war tax receipts. For Paine never doubted, publicly at least, that an independent government would survive the war, and he remarked in the ninth of his *Crisis* papers, on 9 June 1780, that the loss of Charleston would serve only to rekindle 'the blaze of 1776'. Paine ended his paper with the remark that the necessary funds would be raised and that this would demonstrate to England and the world that 'the cause of America stands not on the will of a few but on the broad foundation of property and popularity'.[30] This assertion that the American cause was in the interests of rich and poor alike was a development of an argument he had advanced in the controversy over the Pennsylvania Constitution in December 1778. To those who had opposed a democratic constitution on the grounds that 'it was a good

34

one for the poor man', Paine had replied 'that for that very reason is it the best government for a *rich* one, by producing puchasers, tenants, and labourers, to the landed interest, and consumers to the merchants'.[31] Paine did not deny the existence of class conflicts; he believed, however, that only in a democratic society could they be peacefully and reasonably resolved. If the poor were ignorant, he had gone on to assert, the rich were equally disadvantaged by self-interest, and only a constitution in which all had equal rights would produce a government which would administer in the national interest.[32] This was a point which Paine was to elaborate, with considerable effect, in *Rights of Man*, more than ten years later.

In American domestic politics Paine adhered, in general, to the Jeffersonian position, and when, despite the wishes of President Washington, American democracy developed along party lines, Paine aligned himself with Jefferson and the Republicans against John Adams and the Federalists. Yet, on the issue of federal against state rights, especially on financial policy, Paine was by no means a 'Jeffersonian Democrat'. He first made his position clear in a pamphlet, *Public Good*, which, appearing in December 1780, argued the claims of the Federal government (against those of the state of Virginia) to the virgin lands lying to the west of the Alleghany mountains. In November 1777, Congress had adopted the Articles of Confederation which formally established the authority of Congress, albeit within strict limits, to act on behalf of the 13 colonies. The boundaries of many of these colonies had been defined by the charters under which they had originally been established. Virginia, however, was laying claim to an indefinite extension of her lands to the west; while neighbouring Maryland, whose boundaries were fixed by her charter, was refusing to ratify the Articles of Confederation unless Virginian claims were abandoned. In *Public Good* Paine argued that newly colonised land should be the property of the Federal government until the time came to form new states which would be admitted to the American Union on the same terms as the existing members. Paine saw that the Articles of Confederation, although they were the best arrangement that could be made under existing conditions, were quite unsuitable as the basis for the future American Republic, and he ended his pamphlet by 'renewing a hint which I formerly threw out in the pamphlet "Common Sense" . . . which is that of electing a Continental Convention, defining and describing the powers and authority of Congress'.[33] Paine's proposal met with complete success.[34] Virginia finally abandoned her claim to most of the western territory in dispute; Maryland ratified the Articles of Confederation in March 1781 and on 14 May 1787, the Convention assembled at Philadelphia — the Convention which was to transform the provisional confederation into a federation with a Constitution which survives to the present day.

The issues of federal power and financial policy were clearly linked — a point made forcibly by Washington in a letter of 31 May 1780. 'One State', he complained, 'will comply with a requisition of Congress; another neglects to do it; a third executes it by halves; and all differ either in the manner, the matter, or so much in point of time, that we are always working up hill, and ever shall be; and while such a system as the present one or rather want of one prevails, we shall ever be unable to apply our strength or resources to any advantage.' 'The crisis', he added, 'in every point of view, is extraordinary'[35] — an expression which no doubt inspired the title of a special publication in Paine's *Crisis* series, *The Crisis Extraordinary*, which he completed on 4 October 1780. In this, his approach to financial policy was made very explicit, as was his comprehension of economic issues. Calculating the needs of the federal government at two million pounds a year he proposed raising half the sum by taxes and half by loans at 6½ per cent. As Henry Collins argued, 'Paine would rather have raised the entire sum by taxes but that was out of the question in view of the primitive nature of the government machine.'[36] Paine thought, however, that a million pounds could be raised mainly by import duties, which had the advantage that, since there were only a few points of entry, they would be easy to collect. In an echo from his own past, he also suggested excise duties on liquor. He argued the case with characteristic irony: 'How often have I heard an emphatical wish, almost accompanied, by a tear, "*Oh, that our poor fellows in the field had some of this!*" Why then need we suffer under a fruitless sympathy, when there is a way to enjoy both the wish and the entertainment at once.' He ended his article by linking the questions of federal power and sound finance. He had proposed a regular source of public finance to pay for a standing army in place of the existing system of a part-time militia, which Paine argued was both financially and militarily inefficient. Together with the tax reforms, he supported Congress's proposal for a currency reform. Constant emissions of paper money, inevitable in the early years of war, had depreciated the currency, and Congress was proposing to recall it and issue one unit of new currency for 40 units of old. This, Paine argued, would be administratively convenient — 'Every one knows that I am not the flatterer of Congress, but in this instance they are right; and if that measure is supported, the currency will acquire a value, which, without it, it will not.' Currency reform was, it was true, only a temporary expedient, but it would 'give relief to the finances until such time as they can be properly arranged'.[37]

The immediate effect of *Crisis Extraordinary*, for the printing of which Paine paid from his own pocket, and which was sold to the public below cost, was to convince the Americans of the need to entrust more power to the federal government, and that, pending the creation of a more stable system of war finance, it would be necessary to raise a subsidy or loan from France. Paine wrote personally to Vergennes, the French minister in America, stating the case for French aid, all of which helped to convince Congress that a mission should be sent to France. Washington's aide, Colonel John Laurens, was appointed Envoy Extraordinary, but he was a military expert who knew nothing of politics or finance. He made a special request for Paine to accompany him but there was congressional opposition to Paine being given official status. Animosities which dated from the Silas Deane affair lingered on, and Paine agreed to make the journey at his own expense.[38]

Paine had been hoping, for some months, to visit Europe with a view to crossing the Channel, and conducting subterranean propaganda in England for the American cause. Modesty was never one of Paine's outstanding attributes, and he had written to Greene that 'It was in a great measure owing to my bringing a knowledge of England with me to America that I was enabled to enter deeper into politics, and with more success than other people; and whoever takes the matter up in England must in like manner be possessed of a knowledge of America'.[39] Fortunately Greene was able to persuade his friend that the risk involved was altogether too great, and Paine abandoned the wild scheme. Otherwise he would probably not have survived to compose *Rights of Man*. *Common Sense* was the publication which made Paine famous and its title was also the *nom-de-plume* under which many of his publications, including the *Crisis* papers, appeared. In a way the trade mark was appropriate, since Paine appealed, as no political writer had done before him, to the 'common sense' of ordinary people.

Yet, as a clue to his character, the title was misleading. Paine habitually displayed a good deal more than common sense in his grasp of political issues, and a good deal less in the handling of his private affairs. Moreover, as Franklin's daughter Sarah Bache observed, Paine seemed to go out of his way to dispute with others. 'There never was a man', she wrote to her father, 'less beloved in a place than Payne [*sic*] is in this, having at different times disputed with everybody. The most rational thing he could have done would have been to have died the instant he had finished his Common Sense, for he never again will have it in his power to leave the World with so much credit'.[40]

Partly for these reasons, Paine accompanied Laurens to France, arriving in L'Orient on 9 March and returning from Brest on 1 June. The mission was successful and, while there is no evidence of the part played by Paine in the transactions, Jonathan Williams, America's commercial agent in France, wrote to his grand-uncle, Benjamin Franklin, that 'We agree exceedingly well together, and are growing intimate ... I confess I like him as a companion because he is pleasant as well as a sensible man, and I heartily wish that Party (the anti-Deane Party) had not so good an assistant'.[41]

Either Mrs Bache exaggerated Paine's unpopularity in 1781, or it was short-lived, for early in 1782, it was decided to employ him professionally as a propagandist for Congress. Washington had, for some time, wanted to make some provision for Paine in compensation for his services to the Revolution and, with the complete agreement of the more conservative elements, including Gouverneur Morris, Robert Morris and Robert Livingston, Secretary of Foreign Affairs, Paine was employed at a salary of 800 dollars a year, and supplied with information from government archives.[42] Paine also intended to write a history of the American Revolution, a project which he was never to complete. While working on this, however, he borrowed from Robert Morris a volume by the Abbé Raynal on *The Revolution of America* which had appeared in the previous year. Raynal's book was something of an embarrassment to both the French and American governments, for it argued that the American Revolution was trivial and pointless. In August 1782, Paine published a reply to Raynal in the form of a pamphlet entitled a *Letter to the Abbé Raynal*. Apart from its immediate relevance — and Paine sent 50 copies to General Washington for distribution in the army — it contains much of lasting value and is an admirable expression of Paine's economic and political ideas in the final year of the American Revolution.[43]

Among other things the pamphlet contained an exceptionally clear presentation of the problems of war finance. As Dr Collins described it:

> Inflation and taxation, Paine argued, were alternative ways of paying for war, and taxation was very much to be preferred. However, it required an administrative machine which might not be available to a revolutionary government, so that inflation might be used as a makeshift expedient ... In Paine's view taxation, by directly reducing demand, brought home to people the real costs which their government was incurring and so occasioned 'frugality and thrift', while inflation gave rise to 'dissipation and carelessness.' More to the point, taxation gave governments some control over the allocation of the burden and increased the likelihood that it would be justly distributed. As soon as possible after the end of the war, currency should once again consist of gold and silver so as to restore confidence to the public and an automatic discipline on government.[44]

One of Paine's more recent biographers, Professor Aldridge, states baldly that 'Paine's economics are now outmoded. Virtually a mercantilist, he considered gold and silver as the only form of capital'.[45] But such views are insensitive to the economic circumstances of the time. To quote Dr Collins,

Paine's entire life was passed in a period of secular inflation which began around 1760 when he was twenty-three
and continued until the end of the Napoleonic wars, by
which time he had been dead for five years. In eighteenth-
century conditions money wages nowhere near kept pace
with rising prices, and distress, resulting from inflation,
was to become so acute that the system inaugurated by the
Speenhamland magistrates in England in 1795 of tying
poor relief to bread prices soon spread through much of the
kingdom. To Paine ... the salient feature of inflation was
that it re-distributed income in favour of the rich and to the
detriment of the wage-earner and artisan.[46]

If we consider, too, that Paine spent the most active periods
of his political life in supporting revolutionary governments
which were desperately coping with the inflationary
consequences of war, his ideas can be seen in reasonable
perspective. For while Paine was not entirely free from traces
of mercantilism in his economic thinking, he argued against
paper money and for a gold and silver currency on anti-
inflationary rather than balance-of-payment grounds. On the
other hand, his political ideas were clearly cast in the contemporary mould, and they display the characteristic limitations, as well as the advantages, of the climate deriving from
Locke, Rousseau and the eighteenth-century Enlightenment.[47]

Meanwhile, in the domestic politics of the new American
union, Paine persisted in his attempts to strengthen federal
unity, though his next endeavour, the *Six Letters to Rhode
Island*, was less successful than *Public Good* in persuading an
individual state to subordinate its interests to those of the
wider Confederation. Congressional finances were in their
usual chaotic state and a loan was being negotiated in
Holland, which had joined France and Spain in an alliance of
maritime powers against England. In existing conditions it
was not easy to see how even the interest on the loans was to
be paid, and Congress proposed a 5 per cent import duty
which was generally acceptable. However, under the Articles
of Confederation, a congressional tax required the unanimous
agreement of the states, and one of the 13, Rhode Island, was
clearly going to refuse. Paine's *Six Letters* appeared in the
Providence Gazette between 21 December 1782 and 1 February

1783. They were widely reprinted, though they failed in their objective. Paine argued, as he had previously done, in favour of a system of taxation which would be roughly proportionate to wealth. In wartime America the direct taxation of income or capital wealth was clearly out of the question; Paine supported an import duty on luxuries, for the poor would pay little or nothing while those who consumed such imports would be in a better position to pay tax. Arguing vainly against the exponents of state rights, who were basing their case on Montesquieu's doctrine of separation of powers, Paine wrote that such separation, while a necessary safeguard against tyranny in undemocratic regimes, where the legislature and executives were equally irremovable, was unnecessary and even harmful in conditions where both were elected. Financial stringency had driven Congress to finance the war by a land tax, and while this was a considerable improvement upon the incessant issue of paper money, it had the disadvantage of raising the prices of food and of domestic manufactures, including clothing. On the other hand, the merchant who imported luxuries or semi-luxuries paid no tax, nor did his customer, and it was against this anomaly that Paine directed his proposal.[48]

In April 1783, the War ended and Paine could write in his penultimate *Crisis*: '"The times that tried men's souls" are over — and the greatest and completest revolution the world ever knew, gloriously and happily accomplished.'[49] Now, however, that the government no longer needed his services, his personal position became desperate. On a number of previous occasions, even while the war was in progress, his neglect of his finances had landed him in trouble. He had accepted rather than sought payment for his political and journalistic services. Generous without stint, he seems to have assumed, when he thought about the matter at all, that personal friends or the public authorities whom he had served so well when their cause seemed desperate, would come to his aid in his own time of need. In a memorial which he addressed to a committee of the Continental Congress in October 1783, he referred to the 'many trying and inconvenient situations I have passed over for several years' and referred pointedly to the chagrin he felt 'when I compare what my unvaried conduct and disposition towards the Cause

41

of America has been, and what hers has been to me in return'. The last vice of which Paine could reasonably have been accused was avarice, but he had to live, and it must have been galling to a man of his pride to write 'Trade I do not understand. Land I have none, or what is equal to none. I have exiled myself from one Country without making a home of another'.[50]

Paine was to learn, many times in the course of his life, that there was little gratitude in politics, but the lesson never stuck. There was, according to taste, a touching näiveté or an intolerable conceit about a man who could write, as Paine had written in the thirteenth *Crisis* on the conclusion of the war: 'if, in the course of more than seven years, I have rendered [America] any service, I have likewise added something to the reputation of literature, by freely and disinterestedly employing it in the great cause of mankind, and showing that there may be genius without prostitution'.[51] Though such forthright boasting was rare in Paine's writings, there are enough contemporary accounts of his conversation to establish that he did not hide his light under a bushel. On the other hand, Paine was forthright in everything, and the fact that he was so often right did not reduce the number of his enemies. He made life-long enemies over the Silas Deane affair and he made more, in both Virginia and Rhode Island, by the vigour with which he defended congressional claims against state rights. 'I have never', he could fairly claim in the tenth *Crisis*, 'made it a consideration of whether the subject was popular or unpopular, but whether it was right or wrong.'[52] Luckily for Paine there were many who, like Washington and Jefferson, appreciated his qualities. Jefferson tried to persuade the Virginia Assembly to make Paine a grant of land, but, no doubt remembering Paine's opposition to their State's territorial claims in *Public Good*, the Assembly voted it down. Madison had the grace to write to Washington that 'the world will give us as little credit for our policy as for gratitude in this particular'.[53] Even Washington's personal intervention could only secure Paine a modest cash grant from the Pennsylvania Assembly where his 'conservative' attitude to the bank, and to financial policy in general, had alienated many potential supporters. However, the State of New York gave him, with every sign of enthusiasm, a substantial estate at New

Rochelle, and Congress made him a grant of 3,000 dollars. For a time, at least, he could live in comparative affluence.

By 1786, however, Paine was back in politics, this time to defend the Bank of Pennsylvania, which he had helped to create. The most numerous and vocal of the Bank's critics were the small and middling farmers, who opposed the post-war financial retrenchment and wanted a greater issue of paper currency. In a pamphlet entitled *Dissertations on Government, the Bank, and Paper Money*, Paine replied to the farmers and their supporters by declaring that the role of the Bank was to mobilise savings which would otherwise be unspent, and to return them, through loans, into circulation. In doing so, Paine argued, the Bank would earn its own profits while at the same time serve the interests of the farmers and merchants by increasing the volume of trade, to the benefit of the entire economy. Paine did not use the term 'velocity of circulation' which was to feature so prominently in the later development of monetary theory, but he certainly employed the concept. There was a great deal to his view that, in eighteenth-century conditions, the confidence which was a prerequisite for the expansion of trade and manufacture depended upon a network of sound financial institutions, and upon the imposition, on governments, of an automatic discipline through restricting emission of paper money to the supply of precious metals. However, his views would hardly appeal to the small farmer, in debt to the Bank, who would like to see the real burden of his debt reduced by inflation. For the low-paid wage or salary earner, on the other hand — and Paine could draw on his experience as a customs officer — inflation was often disastrous since his pay would respond slowly, if at all, to rising prices, and its real value would consequently decline.[54]

Paine's vision of an ideal society included not only political democracy but also an expansion of trade and manufacture. This would be made possible by sound finance and also through scientific research. Confidence in science as a means of social amelioration was becoming more common in the eighteenth century, and England, in the 1760s, had seen the rise of such bodies as the Lunar Society of Birmingham in which political radicals, manufacturers, bankers and scholars (the categories often overlapped) met to discuss scientific, technological and social progress. Similar societies began to sprout in America with the coming of peace, and in January 1785, Paine was admitted as a member of the American Philosophical Society of which his friend, Benjamin Franklin, was a leading member. In February 1787, he founded the Society for Political Inquiries, together with Benjamin Franklin, Robert Morris, Gouverneur Morris and Benjamin Rush. On the whole these were two happy and relatively tranquil years in Paine's life, though it would have been too much to expect them to be free from controversy. The stand he took over the Bank of Pennsylvania brought him bitter reproaches from former political allies, some of whom were not above describing him as an unprincipled and hireling author — a charge which left him comparatively unperturbed, as did the accusation, which probably had more foundation, that he drank too much. Now that the Revolution was over, his interest in politics was in abeyance, and when he sailed for France in April 1787, it was mainly to publicise his iron bridge which had the novel if not quite unprecedented feature of being made in segments which could be dismantled, transported and reassembled as necessary.[55]

In May, he arrived at Le Havre with his model, which caused some difficulties at customs but which he displayed to the Academy of Sciences in Paris in July. He was well received in Paris, where his friend Jefferson was now United States minister, and where Lafayette, who had been partly instrumental in securing French aid during the Revolutionary War, received him cordially. In August, he sailed for England to visit his mother, on whom he settled a pension of nine shillings a week, his father having died in the previous year.

It was not long before Paine was back in politics. While in Paris he met, through Lafayette and Jefferson, the radical philosopher Condorçet, and he also corresponded with Cardinal de Brienne, the Archbishop of Toulouse, a leading minister in the government of Louis XVI. Contrary to common impression, Paine was not a doctrinaire republican. While believing in the sovereignty of the people he recognised that the people could be happy under a monarch, and as far as Paine was concerned, the salient characteristic of the French Monarch was the help he had given the American

Revolution, which had made victory possible. As he saw it, France was a country with a mild and open-minded King under whose rule the ideas of the Enlightenment were gaining ground. The worst danger was that of renewed war with England, and it was in relation to this that Paine wrote, probably while he was still in Paris, his next pamphlet, *Prospects on the Rubicon*. Paine knew no French and it was no doubt with the recollection of recent conversations with Condorçet and his friends in mind that he wrote that the French 'were once the freest people in Europe, and ... it is very probable they will be so again. The change is already begun.' 'The people of France', he added, 'are beginning to think for themselves, and the people of England resigning up the prerogative of thinking'.[56]

Paine wrote his pamphlet in an attempt to prevent England from going to war with France. 'Paine was no pacifist', observed Henry Collins,

> But he was against wars waged for dynastic or power-political purposes. He had seen at first hand the misery caused by war; but, while he argued as a humanitarian against the needless infliction of suffering, the main burden of his attack on England's foreign policy was economic and his criticism carried further a line of thought first developed in the United States. England's past wars had increased her national debt and resulted in a heavy load of taxation. But the load was not equally distributed. On the contrary, 'A few men have enriched themselves by jobs and contracts, and the groaning multitude bore the burden.'[57]

Thus far, Paine's case was strong, but he underestimated the economic strength of industrial England; hence the ruin which he predicted as a result of the growing national debt would not come to pass. But Paine had an excuse for his misjudgements in economics. For the past 13 years, he had been out of the country and living in a largely agrarian society. And although he had lived in England for the first 37 years of his life, his experience was mainly confined to Norfolk and Sussex. In 1789, after a visit to the industrial North and Midlands, he was to write to Thomas Jefferson, with a note of some surprise, that 'I have been to see the Cotton Mills, the Potteries, the steel furnaces, white lead manufacture. All those things might be easily carried on in America'.[58] Inevitably, such a simplistic analysis would confound his understanding of the relative economic might of Great Britain.

Paine hoped that his economic arguments would help bring the English to their senses. He arrived in London with a letter from the secretary of Cardinal de Brienne as well as a strong recommendation from Henry Laurens, an old friend of Paine's who had been President of Congress during the Revolutionary War. It seemed only natural that, on his arrival in London, he should present himself to Edmund Burke, a leading Whig who had been an outspoken champion of America since 1774. Through Burke, Paine obtained entry into Whig society. He was a guest at Burke's home and met, on the friendliest of terms, Fox, Shelburne and the Duke of Portland, among other leaders of the Whig opposition. It was Burke who took Paine on his tour of the northern ironworks which so impressed him, and, as relations between England and France grew tense, he kept Jefferson and other American friends informed about political changes in England and their implications for European peace. From his correspondence at the time it is clear that his political views were no more dogmatically republican in relation to England than they were in relation to France, where he continued, up to and beyond the outbreak of the Revolution, to hope for progress from a benevolent monarch advised by enlightened ministers. And while, in view of his American experience, he could hardly regard George III in the same light as Louis XVI, he seems, in general, to have accepted the prevailing Whig view of contemporary English politics.

This emerged very clearly during the Regency crisis which followed the declared insanity of the king in November 1788. Incongruously the Whig opposition stood by the alleged constitutional right of the Prince of Wales to become Regent. Pitt, the Prime Minister, who knew that this would result in his own dismissal in favour of Fox, asserted the right of Parliament to determine the issue. To many it seemed that Pitt was taking the more democratic view in asserting the supremacy of Parliament over the Crown, but Paine, in a letter to Thomas Walker, whose family owned the great iron works near Sheffield, and with whom he was negotiating about his bridge, thought otherwise. In a letter to Walker on 26 February he said that, 'It was one of those cases in which there ought to have been a National Convention elected for the express purpose, for if government be permitted to alter itself, or any of the parts permitted to alter the other there is no fixed Constitution in the country.'

Paine had not yet come round to the view, which he was later to express in *Rights of Man*, to the horror of even some of his radical sympathisers, that England had no constitution. The view expressed in his letter to Walker, two months before the opening stages of the French Revolution, was that England had some sort of constitution, even if a not very satisfactory one, and that 'if the Regal Power, or the person exercising the Regal Power, either as King or Regent, instead of standing on the universal ground of the Nation be made the mere creature of Parliament, it is, in my humble opinion, equally inconsistent and unconstitutional as if Parliament was the mere creature of the Crown'.[59] In a situation in which neither House of Parliament could be said to represent the people, Paine thought 'the conduct of the opposition much nearer to the principles of the Constitution than what the conduct of the Ministry was'. This is hardly Paine at his most penetrating and clear. Returning to England after an absence of 13 years, he had little direct knowledge of the political situation, save what he picked up from his new Whig friends, and it was their views which he was passing on, practically unchanged, to Thomas Walker.

Paine's republicanism, in fact, had been a response — eloquent, powerful and perfectly timed — to the challenge of the American Revolution. Under the stimulus of the Revolutionary War his ideas were constantly developing. Between the Revolutions, while his interest in politics, and particularly in peace, was sustained, his development ceased. As he was later to write to George Washington in a letter of 21 July 1791, he would, after the end of the American War, have settled for a quiet life. Meanwhile, however, the French Revolution occurred and showed him that 'the ardour of Seventy-Six is capable of renewing itself'.[60] A new creative phase in Paine's life and thought was about to unfold.

Notes

1. Quoted in Conway, *Paine*, vol. I, p. 25.
2. Quoted in Aldridge, *Man of Reason*, p. 309.
3. Collins, 'Introduction', p. 13.
4. Paine to Benjamin Franklin, 4 March 1775, *Writings*, vol. II, pp. 1130-2.
5. 'The Magazine in America', *Pennsylvania Magazine* (24 January 1775), *Writings*, vol. II, pp. 1109-13.
6. Hawke, *Paine*, pp. 26-35.
7. 'African Slavery in America', *Pennsylvania Journal* (8 March 1775), *Writings*, vol. II, pp. 15-19.
8. 'A Serious Thought,' *Pennsylvania Journal* (18 October 1775), *Writings*, vol. II, pp. 19-20.
9. 'Duelling', *Pennsylvania Magazine* (May 1775), *Writings*, vol. II, pp. 28-32.
10. 'A Dialogue between General Wolfe and General Gage in a Wood near Boston', *Pennsylvania Journal* (4 January 1775), *Writings*, vol. II, pp. 47-9.
11. 'Thoughts on Defensive War', *Pennsylvania Magazine* (July 1775), *Writings*, vol. II, pp. 52-5.
12. Quoted in Aldridge, *Man of Reason*, p. 34.
13. Collins, 'Introduction', p. 18.
14. Ibid., p. 20.
15. Aldridge, *Man of Reason*, p. 35.
16. Quoted in *Writings*, vol. I, p. 2.
17. Aldridge, *Man of Reason*, p. 43.
18. Collins, 'Introduction', p. 20.
19. See *Writings*, vol. II, p. 60; Aldridge, *Man of Reason*, p. 45.
20. 'The Forester's Letters', *Writings*, vol. II, pp. 61-87.
21. *Crisis* I (13 December 1776), *Writings*, vol. I, pp. 49-57.
22. Quoted in Conway, *Paine*, vol. I, p. 87.
23. 'The Affair of Silas Deane', *Pennsylvania Packet* (31 December 1778-January 1779), *Writings*, vol. II, p. 121.
24. See Hawke, *Paine*, pp. 85-94.
25. 'Emancipation of Slaves' (1 March 1780), *Writings*, vol. II, pp. 21-2.
26. *Crisis* II (13 January 1777), *Writings*, vol. I, pp. 59-60.
27. Collins, 'Introduction', p. 22.
28. See *Writings*, vol. I, p. 165.
29. 'Dissertations on Government' (February 1786), *Writings*, vol. II, pp. 383-4.
30. *Crisis* IX (May 1780), *Writings*, vol. I, pp. 166-70.
31. 'A Serious Address to the People of Pennsylvania', *Pennsylvania Packet* (December 1778), *Writings*, vol. II, pp. 282-3.
32. *Crisis* IX (October 1780), *Writings*, vol. II, pp. 171-88.
33. 'Public Good' (December 1780), *Writings*, vol. II, pp. 303-33.
34. See Hawke, *Paine*, pp. 108-10; Aldridge, *Man of Reason*, p. 85.
35. George Washington, quoted in *Writings*, vol. I, p. 171.

36. Collins, 'Introduction', p. 24.

37. 'The Crisis Extraordinary' (October 1780), *Writings*, vol. I, pp. 171-88. In this discussion Mr Spater was indebted to Dr Collins' 'Introduction', esp. p. 24.

38. See Hawke, *Paine*, pp. 113-20.

39. Paine to Major-General Nathaniel Greene, 9 September 1780, *Writings*, vol. II, pp. 1188-9.

40. Quoted in Aldridge, *Man of Reason*, p. 86.

41. Quoted in ibid., p. 87.

42. Hawke, *Paine*, p. 123.

43. Ibid., pp. 129-32.

44. Collins, 'Introduction', p. 25.

45. Aldridge, *Man of Reason*, p. 121.

46. Collins, 'Introduction', p. 26.

47. 'Letter to the Abbé Raynal' (1782), *Writings*, vol. II, esp. pp. 228-33.

48. 'Six Letters to Rhode Island' (1782-3), *Writings*, vol. II, pp. 333-66.

49. *Crisis* XIII (April 1783), *Writings*, vol. I, p. 230.

50. 'To the Committee of the Continental Congress' (October 1783), *Writings*, vol. II, pp. 1226-8.

51. *Crisis* XIII (April 1783), *Writings*, vol. I, p. 235.

52. *Crisis* X (March 1782), *Writings*, vol. I, p. 196.

53. Quoted in Aldridge, *Man of Reason*, p. 103.

54. 'Dissertations on Government' (February 1786), *Writings*, vol. II, pp. 395-6.

55. See Hawke, *Paine*, pp. 163-4.

56. 'Prospects on the Rubicon' (1787), *Writings*, vol. II, pp. 623-4.

57. Collins, 'Introduction', p. 28.

58. Paine to Thomas Jefferson, 17 June 1789, *Writings*, vol. II, p. 1292.

59. Paine to Thomas Walker, 26 February 1789, *Writings*, vol. II, pp. 1279-80.

60. Paine to George Washington, 21 July 1791, *Writings*, vol. II, p. 1319.

3 European Revolutionary, 1789-1809

George Spater

We have already considered the state of Paine's political outlook when he arrived in America at the end of 1774. The evidence of his *Case of the Officers of the Excise*, which he had written two years earlier, shows that he had acquired, through conversation and reading, the conventional Whig–Radical outlook of the times. But it is fascinating to observe in this pamphlet some of the major themes which were later to feature more prominently in his writings. There was, for instance, the explicit faith in the power of reason to rectify injustice. 'There are some cases', he then wrote, 'so singularly reasonable, that the more they are considered, the more weight they obtain.'[1] He was convinced, just as early in his career, of the evils of inflation, since he attributed the sufferings of his fellow excisemen mainly to 'the increase of money in the kingdom'[2] which had caused prices to rise while the wages of the humbler public servants remained static. There was, finally, the germ of a democratic theory of politics in his suggestion that the remoteness of the rich made them incapable of understanding the problems of poverty. It is not a very large step from here to the conclusion that only by extending the franchise could a legislature be selected which would give proper weight to the grievances of the poor. Paine did not, as yet, draw this conclusion overtly and there is no evidence that he had, as yet, reached it in his own mind. The decisive turn in this regard, as we have seen, was the appearance of *Common Sense* and the *Crisis* papers.

It is impossible to know to what extent Paine's American writings were circulated in England, but we do know that in composing some of them, Paine had an English audience in mind. *Crisis* VI, which appeared in October 1778, warned the English that their country had more to lose than America from a naval blockade. *Crisis* VII (November 1778) was directed explicitly to 'The People of England', and in it Paine laid new stress on the compatability of nationalism and internationalism. 'My attachment', he declared, 'is to all the world, and not to any particular part'.[3] He went on to argue that the present war was not being waged for the benefit of the English common people, but for the 'favourites at court' who would receive grants of conquered land. Politically, too, the war was not in the interests of the people, since victory would give the Crown a source of income independent of Parliament. Democracy and prosperity alike would gain by the King's defeat.[4] Finally, in October 1782, as the war was nearing its end, Paine addressed *Crisis* XII to the new Prime Minister, the Earl of Shelburne, urging him to ease the burden on the English worker by suing for peace.[5]

Between 1787, when he returned from America, and 1789, Paine spent most of his time commuting between Paris and London, concerning himself with his iron bridge and the prospects of an Anglo-French war. When the Estates-General convened at Versailles on 5 May 1789, Paine was still in England, where he remained until September. He did not, therefore, experience at first hand the transformation of the Estates-General into the National Assembly on 17 June, nor did he witness the fall of the Bastille on 14 July. For information on these developments, as well as on the abolition of feudal rights on 4 August, and the 'Declaration of the Rights of Man and of Citizen' on 26 August, he relied on correspondence with his friends in France, especially Thomas Jefferson. Paine was still in London on 18 September when he replied to a letter from Jefferson. This reply, which shows that Paine knew no more than anyone else how the Revolution would develop, was probably a fair summary of attitudes in England towards the Revolution, then in its third month. 'The people of this country', he declared, 'speak very differently on the affairs of France':

> The mass of them so far as I can collect say that France is a much freer country than England. The press, the Bishops etc., say the National Assembly has gone too far. There is yet in this country very considerable remains of the feudal system which people did not see before the revolution in France [placed] it before their eyes. While the multitudes here could be terrified with the cry and apprehension of arbitrary power, wooden shoe, popery, and such like stuff, they thought themselves by comparison extraordinary free people. But the bug-bear now loses its force, and they appear to me to be turning their eyes toward the aristocrats of their own nation. There is a new mode of conquering and I think it will have its effect. I am looking out for a place to erect my bridge ...[6]

Paine's account of the movement of opinion in England was accurate as far as it went. There was a small but significant groundswell in response to the French Revolution among both the aristocratic Friends of the People, led by such Whigs as Fox and Grey, who had welcomed the fall of the Bastille in ecstatic terms, and the largely Nonconformist Revolution Society, which had celebrated, on 4 November 1788, the centenary of the English Revolution, and which a year later issued a congratulatory 'Address to the French National Assembly'. In September 1789 Paine crossed the Channel to witness at first hand the developments which promised to extend the rule of liberty and reason in France, and so, in the words of the Revolution Society, 'to encourage other nations to assert the unalienable rights of mankind, and thereby to introduce a general reformation in the governments of Europe, and to make the world free and happy'.[7] Dr Richard Price, a leading member of the Revolution Society, spoke for a substantial section of democratic opinion when, in his *Discourse on the Love of Our Country,* he interpreted these 'unalienable rights' to include 'the right to liberty of conscience in religious matters', 'the right to resist power when abused' and 'the right to choose our own governors; to cashier them for misconduct; and to frame a government for ourselves'.[8]

Late in 1789 Paine left for France with no notion of either the future development of the French Revolution or of the strength and ferocity of the conservative reaction which would develop against it in England. However, from now on Paine was in direct contact with the Revolution, and especially with the group which had drawn up, in August, the Declaration of the Rights of Man and of Citizen.[9] It is not clear how directly Paine's detailed advice was sought in drawing up the new liberal constitution, but he was certainly close to the Lafayette circle which included many who subsequently became leaders of the Girondin faction. It was decided that, for the second time, Paine's propagandist talents would be enlisted in the service of a revolution, and on 12 January 1790, Lafayette wrote to Washington that *'Common sense* is writing for you a brochure in which you will see a portion of my adventures. The result will be, I hope, happy for my country and for humanity'.[10] In March, Paine decided to return to England in connection with his iron bridge, which Walkers of Rotherham had agreed to assemble. 'I take with me to London', he told an anonymous friend in Philadelphia, 'the key to the Bastile [sic], which the Marquis [de Lafayette] entrusts to my care as his present to General Washington.[11] The key, declared Paine, symbolised 'the first ripe fruits of American principles transplanted into Europe'.[12]

On his return to England Paine was shocked to read of Burke's violent attack on the French Revolution in his speech to the House of Commons on 9 February. The two men had been on friendly terms since Paine's arrival in England in 1787. Since 1775, Burke had been considered the greatest British supporter of America's cause. Moreover, Burke was clearly impressed with Paine from their first meeting, and in the summer of 1788 he had written to John Wilkes: 'I am just going to dine with the Duke of Portland, in company with the great American Paine.'[13] On 6 January of the following year, Paine wrote to an American friend on the occasion of her marriage: 'As it happens, I am in pretty close intimacy with the heads of the opposition — the Duke of Portland, Mr. Fox and Mr. Burke.'[14]

Burke's attack on the French Revolution seemed to Paine a bewildering betrayal of the reform cause. But Burke was not new to conservative politics. As early as 1782, in a speech on reform of representation in the House of Commons, he had made his position abundantly clear by declaring that 'a nation is not an idea only of local extent, and individual momentary aggregation; but it is an idea of continuity, which extends in time as well as in numbers, and in space'.[15] And in his speech of 9 February 1790, Burke showed how it was possible consistently to uphold the 'Glorious Revolution' of 1688 in England, while denouncing the revolution 100 years later in France. 'We did not', he rightly argued, 'impair the monarchy. Perhaps it might be shown that we strengthened it very considerably. The nation kept the same ranks, the same orders, the same privileges, the same franchises, the same rules for property.'[16]

Similarly, the American Revolution had constituted no social upheaval and the only property forfeited was that of American Tories who supported the English cause. By contrast, the French Revolution had abolished feudal property as early as 4 August 1789, and it was manifestly undermining, even before it eventually abolished, the institution of monarchy. It is ironic that Burke should have perceived, much sooner than Fox or Paine, the nature of the forces which the French Revolution had unleashed.

Burke's *Reflections on the Revolution in France*, which appeared in November 1790, was merely a systematic development of views that he had long held and expressed. In Burke's view, as Henry Collins observed,

> society is a developing, organic, mystic entity, and continuity is of its essence. [He] conceded that from time to time reforms would be needed, while exceptional and desperate circumstances might even justify an upheaval. But the object of any such change should be to conserve and not disrupt the essential continuity of the nation.[17]

'A state without the means of some change is without the means of its conversation',[18] Burke had maintained. And it might, very exceptionally, as in 1688, be necessary to overthrow a king who, like James II, was charged 'with nothing less than a design, confirmed by a multitude of illegal overt acts, to *subvert the Protestant church and state*'.[19] But the claim of Dr Price and the Revolution Society was that all government not resting on popular consent was invalid. Equally untenable, according to Burke, was the view that the people had the right, at any time, 'To frame a government for themselves'. No such right existed, he argued, because 'Each contract of each particular state is but a clause in the great primaeval contract of eternal society, linking the lower with the higher natures, connecting the visible and invisible world.' Government, once established, became 'a partnership not only between those who are living, but between those who are living, those who are dead, and those who are to be born'.[20]

Paine's reply, *Rights of Man* Part I, appeared in London in February 1791. It was the first of many replies from leading Radicals of the day, but it was outstandingly the most thorough and the most effective. Of the others, the best known was Sir James Mackintosh's *Vindiciae Gallicae*, which was completed in April, but on 1 August Burke wrote to a friend that 'I have not read, or even seen Mackintosh. But Rickhard tells me, that it is Paine at bottom'; and he added that all his other critics appeared to be 'Paine with some difference in the way of stating'.[21]

Paine's pamphlet appeared at first in small numbers, for sufficient pressure was exerted on his publisher to persuade him to abandon the project.[22] The first substantial edition appeared in March, with the assistance of Thomas Holcroft, Thomas Hollis and William Godwin, the anarchist philosopher whose *Political Justice* was to appear in 1793.[23] Paine's pamphlet was issued at the comparatively high price of three shillings, and although government action to suppress the pamphlet was suggested almost immediately in the *Critical Review* (March 1791), the government, at least for the time being, opted to do no more than commission a writer named George Chalmers 'to rummage in Paine's past and print whatever dirt he could turn up'.[24] Perhaps this alone would silence Paine; besides, at three shillings a copy, the pamphlet might prove to be without serious political effect.

Doubtless the Pitt government was also consoled by the hostile replies to Paine in the public press. One of the first of these — an anonymous tract entitled *Remarks on Mr. Paine's*

Pamphlet called the Rights of Man, published in Dublin in 1791 — expressed alarm at the decision of the 'Whigs of the Capital' (the Constitutional Society in London) to disseminate the work. The writer complained, three years before the appearance of *The Age of Reason,* about Paine's suggestion that the Old Testament might not be divinely inspired. Another ground for complaint was Paine's attack on hereditary monarchy. If this were conceded, the critic argued, the attack could be extended to hereditary property — and, indeed, with the appearance of *Agrarian Justice* in 1794, it was. In 1791 a pamphlet by 'A Barrister' attacked Paine's central contention that no generation could be bound by the decisions of its predecessors. He argued that generations were not discrete entities — it was not possible to say where one left off and its successor began — so that man, as Burke had contended, was born inheriting a web of social institutions and obligations. Moreover, said 'Barrister', even if one accepted Paine's position regarding the inherent rights of a generation to reconstitute its political and social institutions as it saw fit, the wisdom of so doing was even more problematical, and Paine drew no distinction between the two. A third booklet, appearing in the same year, entitled *A Defence of the Constitution of England against the Libels that have been lately published on it: particularly in Paine's Pamphlet on the Rights of Man,* agreed that Burke and Paine were equally one sided in their attitude towards the French Revolution. However, Burke, at least, wanted to protect his country from 'the evils of anarchy', which it was the intention of 'the American Spy, *Mr. Thomas Paine*', to unleash.

Meanwhile, Paine, back in Paris, was engaged in his second round of republican agitation. He renewed his contact with Condorçet, who in 1789 had helped to initiate Paine into the intellectual and political life of the French capital. It is impossible to identify or to disentangle the influence which such men as Condorçet, Paine and Godwin mutually exerted upon one another. But the evidence points to a significant intellectual relationship among them, and to a common stock of ideas developing from Locke and the English Revolution, through France and the Enlightenment, to America through Franklin and Paine, and back to England, through a large number of channels, including Paine and Godwin. As they saw it, man was naturally good, and political authority a necessary (though in Godwin's case an unnecessary) evil. Man depended on society, but was corrupted by it, and in particular by tyrannical authority buttressed by religious superstition and by political and economic privilege. War between nations was an expression of monarchical ambition, as well as a source of suffering for the poor. The emphasis would differ between one writer and another, but in France, America and England this social philosophy was becoming increasingly prevalent. And in the mind of Paine, at least, the radical creeds of republicanism, freethought and hostility towards economic and social privilege were becoming more and more blended.[25]

On his return to Paris, Paine helped to establish, together with Condorçet, de Bonneville, DuChastelet and possibly Brissot, a republican society with a handful of members. Meanwhile, the republican cause received a great impetus when the King and his family, recently fleeing Paris to join the Royalist forces in Metz, were caught at Varennes and brought back to Paris by force on 20 June. In the eyes of large numbers of Parisians the episode transformed the King from an innocent victim of corrupt advisers into a traitor. On 1 July a manifesto, largely written by Paine and translated by DuChastelet, appeared on the walls of Paris demanding the proclamation of a republic. Though signed by DuChastelet, as a French citizen, the manifesto was widely known to be the work of Paine. The Abbé Sieyès, who still supported the idea of a constitutional monarchy, replied to Paine, and a lively public debate ensued. With Paine's full and public participation it helped to turn opinion in favour of a republican solution.[26]

On 13 July Paine returned to London, only to find his quarrel with Burke at the centre of public attention. Immediately he involved himself with the Society for Constitutional Information, which had already released the *Rights of Man* in a cheap edition. Within the Society Paine's circle of friends included Horne Tooke, a leading member of the Society, 'Clio' Rickman, who was later to write a biography of Paine, Dr Joseph Priestley, whose scientific experiments (which included the accidental discovery of oxygen) interested Paine as much as his radical ideas, the artist and mystic, William

Blake, and William Godwin and his future wife, Mary Wollstonecraft.[27] Paine wrote, and Horne Tooke signed, a widely distributed *Address and Declaration* which welcomed the French Revolution 'for having laid the axe to the root of tyranny, and erecting government on the sacred *hereditary rights of man*'. The *Address* went on to argue that 'every nation has at all times, an inherent, indefeasible right to constitute and establish such government for itself, as best accords with its disposition, interest and happiness'.[28]

From July onwards the debate which had begun between Burke and Paine developed on a nationwide scale. At the same time, to be on the safe side, the government was stepping up its repression. The adoption of the *Address and Declaration*, which was scheduled for a meeting at the Crown and Anchor on 4 August (the second anniversary of the abolition of feudal rights in France) had to be postponed until 20 August, when it took place in the Thatched House Tavern. The first meeting, as the *Address and Declaration* made clear, had been 'prevented by the interference of certain *unnamed* and *skulking* persons with the master of the tavern'. Coming less than a month after the Birmingham riots of 14 July, the apprehensions of the proprietor of the Crown and Anchor are partly understandable.[29] In some parts of the country Paine was already being burned in effigy, and, after he became known as the author of the *Address and Declaration*, he was increasingly treated, by both sides, as the living embodiment of the values of the French Revolution.

Paine had no allusions about the state of public opinion. In November 1791 he informed John Hall, whom he had employed to help him with his scientific work in Philadelphia, that 'At present I am engaged on my political Bridge. I shall bring out a new work soon after New Year. It will produce something one way or another. I see the tide is yet the wrong way, but there is a change of sentiment beginning.' He estimated the sales of *Rights of Man* in England at 16,000; in Ireland over 40,000; in Scotland 1,000.[30] Later, in July 1792, he would hand a thousand pounds of his profits to the Constitutional Society, while subsequent editions of the *Rights of Man* would be sold at cost. As usual, Paine did not wish to make money from his publications; he had already outsold Burke, which was satisfaction in itself.[31]

On 16 February 1792, Paine published Part II of *Rights of Man*. Whereas in Part I he was concerned with defending the French Revolution and with analysing the general principles of government, he was concerned in Part II with detailing an innovative (if not seditious) programme of social welfare which would foreshadow the British welfare institutions of the twentieth century. Part II, as was to be expected, enjoyed the same astounding success as Part I, and by the end of the year the two volumes had combined sales of about 200,000. At last the government took recourse to legal action, and on 21 May 1792, Paine was served with a summons to stand trial for his 'wicked and seditious writings'.[32]

On 8 June Paine appeared before the Court of King's Bench, but to his considerable disappointment, the trial was postponed until 18 December. Throughout the summer Paine lived with his friend 'Clio' Rickman; he also sat for his portrait by Romney (now in the National Portrait Gallery, London) and quietly composed his most revolutionary pronouncement to date — the *Letter Addressed to the Addressers on the Late Proclamation*. It was directed in the first instance to 'the numerous rotten boroughs and corporation addresses' which had appeared in support of the government's proclamation against seditious writings. While there was room for doubt as to the seditiousness of *Rights of Man* Part II, there was no ambiguity whatever about the *Letter Addressed to the Addressers*, which called for a popular convention, elected by the people, to draft a new and republican constitution for England. The *Letter*, by calling openly for revolution, made Paine's conviction certain in any English court. Fortunately for him he was in Paris when it appeared, having been elected to the Convention, and all his increasingly numerous enemies could do was to burn him in effigy, which they did with growing enthusiasm throughout November and December. In the latter month Paine was declared outside the law; never again would he set foot in his native country.[33]

Paine's worst enemy (and there would have been stiff competition for the title) could never charge him with being a time-server. In 1783, he had remarked 'I have never yet made, and I hope I never shall make, it the least point of consideration, whether a thing is *popular* or *unpopular*, but whether it is *right* or *wrong*',[34] and he lived up to his principle in the fullest and most literal sense. His friends in Paris, such as Condorçet and Brissot, were associated with the Girondin faction, and the leading Girondins were in prison by the beginning of June 1793. Even before this, Paine had annoyed the Jacobins by voting against the execution of the King. Henry Collins suggested three grounds on which Paine did so:

> As a humanitarian he opposed the taking of life unless it was unavoidable; as an American he could not forget that the France of Louis XVI had been America's ally during the revolutionary war; finally, Paine was too good a propagandist not to realize what the King's execution would do to the reputation of France.[35]

Moreover, Paine spoke little French. In the American Revolution and the English radical movement his ideas could develop in direct and personal contact with people and events. In France he could only see things through spectacles provided by his Girondin friends, and while they may have been excellent guides in philosophy and politics under the old regime, they were soon out of their depth in the turmoil of the French Revolution. After the King's execution in January 1793, France felt more than ever like a beleaguered fortress, surrounded by enemies; Paris itself was feverish and unpredictable. Paine had played some part in the discussions of a committee set up to draft a new constitution, but his contributions were undistinguished, and the committee ineffectual.

On 10 July 1793 the Committee of Public Safety was formed, and on 13 July the revolutionary leader Marat was assassinated. For another year Robespierre was to remain in power. The lives of all suspects were in danger; and almost everyone was a suspect. Paine was especially vulnerable; he was an Englishman, and England had been at war with France since February. And, since he had tried to save the King's life, it was inevitable in the prevailing atmosphere that he should be suspected of monarchial sympathies. After 2 June he had ceased to attend meetings of that Convention, and on 28 December he was arrested and imprisoned in the Luxembourg.

Six hours before his arrest, Paine had completed the first part of his next major work, *The Age of Reason*, and he handed the material to his friend Joel Barlow to arrange for publication. Much earlier in the year he had completed the manuscript of a work on religion which had been translated into French, and which the Jacobin government had promptly suppressed. The irrepressible Paine immediately resumed work on the same theme. Many years later he was to write to Samuel Adams that 'I saw my life in continual danger. My friends were falling as fast as the guillotine could cut their heads off, and as I every day expected the same fate, I resolved to begin my work.' Though *The Age of Reason* was to raise a storm of protest among the pious, it is important to bear in mind the purpose for which it was written. In the same letter Paine explained that 'the people of France were running headlong into atheism, and I had the work translated and published in their own language to stop them in that career, and fix them to the first article (as I have before said) of every man's creed who has any creed at all, *I believe in God.*'[36]

The first edition of *The Age of Reason* appeared while Paine was still in the Luxembourg. Unfortunately for him, Gouverneur Morris, his old enemy since the days of the Silas Deane affair, was American Ambassador in Paris, and his efforts to secure Paine's release, as an American citizen, were perfunctory. It was not until Morris had been replaced by James Monroe that any serious efforts were made on his behalf, and these remained ineffective until some months after the fall of Robespierre, when Paine was finally released on 4 November 1794.

During his nine months in prison, when the reign of terror was at its height, Paine did not know from one day to the next whether he would be guillotined. This frightful uncertainty undermined his health. Monroe took Paine into his home, where he lived for at least a year, and where Mrs Monroe nursed him through a critical illness. During his sojourn with the Monroes, in the *Rue de Richelieu*, Paine wrote Part II of *The Age of Reason*, completing his attack on Christianity, along with all other kinds of revealed religion, and defending his own version of Deistic-Humanism. Although it was not one of his more original works, *The Age of Reason* was to be one of Paine's most influential. A wing of the radical movement through much of the nineteenth century, which combined political republicanism with philosophical anti-clericalism and freethought, published and read Paine's *Rights of Man* and *The Age of Reason* as two of their basic texts.

Soon after his release, Paine was readmitted to the Convention. At the same time, he was actively engaged in furthering the interests of international democracy. The defeat of England in her counter-revolutionary war, he was convinced, would benefit all humanity, including the English people themselves.

In 1796 Paine returned to the theme of England's economy, writing and publishing a pamphlet entitled *The Decline and Fall of the English System of Finance*. France, like America, said Paine, had resorted to inflation, through the issue of paper money, to cover current expenses. Such a policy, though harmful, was unavoidable in time of war, and the harm was immediately apparent through rising prices. On the other hand the English system of financing wars through borrowing was attended with more disastrous consequences. Admittedly it withdrew purchasing power to cover government spending, and so dampened some of the immediate inflationary effects of war, but in the long run it lifted the National Debt out of sight of the gold reserves. Within two decades, Paine predicted, the British system would collapse. Every expansion of the national debt increased the load of interest payments which could only be met by further depreciating the currency. Like the law of gravitation, he claimed, the process accelerated in geometric ratio. Paine was convinced that he had stumbled on a new economic law of epoch-making importance. 'I have not *made* the ratio', he insisted, 'any more than Newton made the ratio of gravitation. I have only discovered it, and explained the mode of applying it'.[37]

In terms of economic analysis the *Decline and Fall* was highly deficient. Again Paine underestimated the inner strength of England's industrial economy. However, as propaganda the *Decline and Fall* helped to sustain French morale during the French Revolutionary Wars. Moreover, the Directory, which had taken control of French affairs after the fall of Robespierre, regarded it as sufficiently important to ensure its appearance in five other countries besides France, including England and America.[38]

Paine was not yet completely spent as a revolutionary writer, but nearly so. England was no longer his home, and even America was turning against him. There, the *Rights of Man* had divided public opinion along much the same lines as it had in England. During the Presidency of Washington a two-party system had developed, and antagonism between the conservative Federalists, led by John Adams, and the more radical Republicans, led by Thomas Jefferson, had become acute. The Federalists were afraid that the egalitarian principles of the French Revolution might spread to America. One of the earliest American attacks on Paine's pamphlet had appeared in a series of letters to the *Columbian Sentinel* of Boston, by John Quincy Adams, using the pseudonym 'Publicola'. The letters were reprinted in 1793 in London as *An Answer to Pain's [sic] Rights of Man*.[39] According to Adams and the American Federalists, the American Revolution had been fought for independence, not equality. What the new Republic now needed was a strong central government based on the eternal principles of civilisation, which included respect for both property and precedent. The spirit of radical and egalitarian innovation expounded in *Rights of Man* was an infection which should, as far as possible, be kept out of the New World. John Quincy Adams, like many English conservatives, was embarrassed by Burke's vehemence and hysteria. Burke and Paine, he declared, had been equally one-sided in their treatment of the French Revolution. Nevertheless, on all the central issues, Adams was on the side of Burke. 'This principle', he argued, 'that a whole nation has a right to do whatever it pleases, cannot in any sense whatever be admitted as true. The eternal and immutable laws of justice and of morality are paramount to all human legislation'.[40]

On this, Adams spoke for a powerful section of the American public which reacted to the French Revolution with alarm and hostility. By 1793, Paine, for his uncompromising defence of that revolution, was already in bad repute with American conservatives; and the appearance of *The Age of Reason* in 1794 added considerably to the number of his enemies among the devout members of all Christian denominations. As though determined to do everything he could to increase his unpopularity, Paine wrote, against the urgent advice of James Monroe and of other American friends in Paris, a *Letter to*

George Washington in July 1796. In it, he gave full vent to his bitterness at Washington's failure to intervene effectively on his behalf during his sojourn in the Luxembourg. Had Washington, during the grim ten months in which Paine was in constant danger of execution, claimed him as an American citizen and requested his release, the French government might well have felt obliged to comply. As it was, with Paine an outlaw in his native country, which of course was at war with France, he was virtually stateless and without protection.

It need not be asked here to what extent America's lamentable treatment of Paine was due to the malevolence of Gouverneur Morris, the moral cowardice of Washington, or a combination of both. Paine's feelings were understandable and his language had lost none of its vigour. After recalling their earlier camaraderie throughout the Revolutionary War, Paine reminded the President that 'After the Revolution of America was established I ventured into the new scenes of difficulties to extend the principles which that Revolution had produced, and you rested at home to partake of the advantages. In the progress of events, you beheld yourself a President in America, and me a prisoner in France. You folded your arms, forgot your friend and became silent'.[41] In his *Letter* Paine placed Washington's whole career under unfavourable review, including his wartime generalship, which Paine had so warmly commended at the time. The importance of the *Letter* was mainly to ensure that Paine's enemies were not confined to readers of the *Rights of Man* and *The Age of Reason*.

During the winter of 1795-6, while still a guest of the Monroes', Paine wrote the manuscript of what was to be his last major political work. Like everything he wrote, it was a direct response to an immediate political challenge. The Directory, which with difficulty was retaining control of revolutionary France, was under fire from left and right. The royalists were working for the restoration of the old regime while from the left came a demand that the political equality for which the revolution stood should be accompanied by economic equality based on the common ownership of land. In February 1796 the Directory closed many of the dissident clubs, mainly royalist, but also the republican Club Pantheon.

In May 1796 Gracchus Babeuf and his principal followers were arrested for conspiring to seize power and inaugurate a communist regime. In January 1797 a royalist *coup* was similarly forestalled by discovery and arrests. After this, Paine decided to publish his pamphlet in French, and later in the same year it appeared in English, under the title *Agrarian Justice opposed to Agrarian Law, and to Agrarian Monopoly.*[42]

Paine's object in publishing an English edition of *Agrarian Justice* was to counter the criticisms of the Bishop of Llandaff to *The Age of Reason*. In particular Paine took issue with the Bishop's suggestion that God in his 'Wisdom and Goodness' had 'made both rich and poor'. To Paine this was nonsense: 'It is wrong to say God made *rich* and *poor*; He made only *male* and *female*; and He gave them the earth for their inheritance.' Paine had a further message for the clergy:

> Instead of preaching to encourage one part of mankind in insolence ... it would be better that priests employed their time to render the condition of man less miserable than it is. Practical religion consists in doing good; and the only way of serving God is that of endeavoring to make His creation happy. All preaching that has not this for its object is nonsense and hypocrisy.

Paine's politics and religion were intertwined in *Agrarian Justice*. God had provided man with land, but He had not intended that it be accumulated in large quantities by a small section of society. Moreover, personal property 'is, in many instances, the effect of paying too little for the labour that produced it; the consequence of which is, that the working hand perishes in old age, and the employer abounds in affluence'. God would not sanction such robbery, Paine argued; therefore, 'of personal property beyond what a man's own hands produce ... he owes on every principle of justice ... a part of the accumulation back again to society'. Having established his principle, Paine proceeded to propose an inheritance tax of 10 per cent to help finance a cash grant of £15 to everyone on attaining the age of 21, and an annual pension of £10 to people over the age of 50.[43]

Agrarian Justice was Paine's last great political work. He was 60 when it appeared in English translation, and the last twelve years of his life were spent, for the most part, in near oblivion. In the spring of 1797, soon after the recall of Monroe to the United States, Paine moved into lodgings with Nicolas de Bonneville and his family. De Bonneville was an old friend and colleague who had published the translation of the first French edition of *Rights of Man* Part II, in 1792. Paine continued to play an active part in French political life, though his ability to influence events was markedly reduced. In 1798 he formed part of a lively social circle which included such Irish revolutionary *émigrés* as Napper Tandy and Wolfe Tone. Paine actively urged the Directory and General Bonaparte to invade England and liberate its people.[44]

Paine was increasingly unhappy and anxious to return to America, his real home since 1774. So long as John Adams remained President, however, he could be sure of an unwelcoming reception. But upon the accession of Thomas Jefferson to the presidency in 1801, conditions were different. More loyal to his friends than George Washington, Jefferson offered Paine a relatively safe passage in a US government ship, an act of generosity which Jefferson's Federalist opponents exploited to the fullest. As it happened, Paine delayed his departure until the Treaty of Amiens brought about a short-lived peace between England and France. He now had no need for American protection, and on 1 September 1802 he sailed from France.

On 30 October Paine arrived at Baltimore. His reception was overwhelmingly unfriendly. It was over a quarter of a century since *Common Sense* and the first of the *Crisis* papers had begun to galvanise American political opinion. The War had been over for 20 years. What was remembered was not Paine's services to the Revolution but his attacks on orthodox Christianity and on George Washington, who was venerated, even by his political opponents, as 'father of the nation'. Paine was confident that in the federal Capital he would find friends. Jefferson gave him open house in Washington, and three other ministers — the acting Vice-President and the Secretaries of the Treasury and of War — entertained him hospitably, although the Federalists kept up their attacks with persistent venom, identifying Jefferson with the notorious subversive and infidel whom he befriended.[45]

Paine soon resumed his political activities — indeed nothing but death could stop him. During his last years in France, he and his friend de Bonneville had fallen foul of Napoleon, who had seized power from the Directory, as First Consul, in 1799. It was, in part, the harassment of Napoleon's police that convinced Paine to return to America at the first opportunity. But his experience did nothing to diminish his interest in France, and in 1802, when Franco–American relations reached their nadir over the acquisition of the former Spanish colony of Louisiana, Paine attacked the Federalists, who were demanding the seizure of the disputed territory. He fully supported his friend Monroe in his mission, which culminated in the purchase of Louisiana from Napoleon. Paine also attacked the Federalists for nepotism under the Adams administration, contrasting their practices unfavourably with those of the Jefferson regime with its dedication to democracy and peace.

Paine's journalistic services to the Republicans continued almost until his death. His last known article appeared on 25 August 1808, in which he attacked the Federalists once again for their anti-French policy. This, Paine argued, would be harmful to the expansion of American commerce, particularly after peace had been restored in Europe.

During these last years of his life, in which the sickness brought on by his imprisonment in the Luxembourg began to exact an increasing toll, Paine lived in increasing self-neglect. His circle of friends grew narrower, his journalistic output, though nearly always of a high calibre by any normal standards, grew more repetitive. With age and illness, his greatness was over, and the less pleasing side of his nature, which included vanity and an uncertain temper, grew more apparent. Throughout his life he had shown some ineptitude in handling his own personal and financial affairs, and some of the troubles which clouded his last years were self-inflicted. But without doubt, most of his suffering stemmed from the malice of political and religious opponents.

When, feeling the end approaching, Paine asked to be buried in a Quaker cemetery, he had his last, sad experience with Christian charity. 'I know not', he wrote in the will drawn up shortly before his death, 'if the Society of people called Quakers, admit a person to be buried in their burying ground, who does not belong to their Society, but if they do, or will admit me, I would prefer being buried there; my father belonged to that profession, and I was partly brought up in it. But if it is not consistent with their rules to do this, I desire to be buried on my own farm at New Rochelle'.[46] The Quakers of New York found it inconsistent with their rules and Paine was buried on his farm.

Madame de Bonneville, who had accompanied Paine on his return journey to the United States, described the burial as 'a scene to affect and to wound any sensible heart':

> Contemplating who it was, what man it was, that we were committing to an obscure grave on an open and dis-regarded bit of land, I could not help feeling most acutely. Before the earth was thrown down upon the coffin, I, placing myself at the east end of the grave, said to my son Benjamin, 'Stand you there, at the other end, as a witness for grateful America.' Looking around me, and beholding the small group of spectators, I exclaimed, as the earth was tumbled into the grave, 'Oh! Mr. Paine! My son stands here as testimony of the gratitude of America, and I, for France!'[47]

In 1819, a political refugee in the USA, William Cobbett, collected Paine's bones and took them back to England. On Cobbett's death, in 1835, they passed to his heirs. After that, they become difficult to trace.

Notes

1. 'Case of the Officers' (1772), *Writings*, vol. II, p. 4.
2. Ibid., p. 5.
3. *Crisis* VII (21 November 1778), *Writings*, vol. II, p. 146.
4. *Writings*, vol. II, p. 151.
5. *Crisis* XII (29 October 1782), *Writings*, vol. II, pp. 221-9.
6. Paine to Thomas Jefferson, 18 September 1789, *Writings*, vol. II, p. 1296.
7. Quoted in Albert Goodwin, *The Friends of Liberty: The English Democratic Movement in the Age of the French Revolution* (London: Hutchinson, 1979), p. 111.
8. Quoted in D.O. Thomas, *The Honest Mind: The Thought and Work of Richard Price* (Oxford: The Clarendon Press, 1977), pp. 299-301.
9. Collins, 'Introduction', p. 30.
10. Quoted in Aldridge, *Man of Reason*, pp. 126-7.

11. Paine to Anonymous Friend, 16 March 1790, *Writings*, vol. II, p. 1285. Dr Foner incorrectly dates the letter 1789.

12. Paine to George Washington, 1 May 1790, *Writings*, vol. II, p. 1303.

13. Quoted in Aldridge, *Man of Reason*, p. 129.

14. Paine to Kitty Nicolson Few, 6 February 1789, *Writings*, vol. II, p. 1276.

15. Speech on 'Representation of the Commons in Parliament' (7 May 1782), *The Works of the Right Honourable Edmund Burke* (London: C. and J. Rivington, 1826), vol. X, p. 97.

16. 'Substance of the Speech of the Right Honourable Edmund Burke' (9 February 1790), p. 29 (University of Saskatchewan, Special Collections, AC 901 A2 B95).

17. Collins, 'Introduction', p. 31.

18. *Reflections on the Revolution in France* (1790), ed. Conor Cruise O'Brien (Harmondsworth: Penguin, 1968), p. 106.

19. Ibid., p. 113.

20. Ibid., pp. 106, 113, 119-22, 194-5.

21. R.R. Fennessy, *Burke, Paine and the Rights of Man* (The Hague: M. Nijhoff, 1963), p. 211. Partly quoted in Collins, 'Introduction', p. 33.

22. Hawke, *Paine*, p. 223.

23. Ibid., p. 223.

24. Ibid., p. 225.

25. Mr Spater intended to expand upon this theme, but his work on the Enlightenment context of Paine's thought was not far advanced at the time of his death.

26. See Hawke, *Paine*, pp. 228-9.

27. On Paine's ambiguous relations with the Society, see ibid., pp. 206-7.

28. Quoted in Goodwin, *Friends of Liberty*, pp. 184-5.

29. See ibid., p. 185.

30. Paine to John Hall, 25 November 1791, *Writings*, vol. II, pp. 1321-2.

31. See Hawke, *Paine*, p. 250.

32. Ibid., p. 248; Aldridge, *Man of Reason*, p. 161.

33. Hawke, *Paine*, pp. 253-5, 267-70; Goodwin, *Friends of Liberty*, p. 263.

34. 'Six Letters to Rhode Island', Letter V (16 January 1783), *Writings*, vol. II, p. 360.

35. Collins, 'Introduction', p. 38.

36. Paine to Samuel Adams, 1 January 1803, *Writings*, vol. II, p. 1436.

37. *The Decline and Fall of the English System of Finance* (1796), *Writings*, vol. II, p. 657.

38. Collins, 'Introduction', p. 41; *Writings*, vol. II, p. 651.

39. See Hawke, *Paine*, pp. 234-5; Conway, *Paine*, vol. I, pp. 292-4.

40. 'Letters of Publicola', Letter II, *Columbian Centinel* (11 June 1791), *The Writings of John Quincy Adams*, ed. Worthington C. Ford (New York: Macmillan, 1913), vol. I, p. 70.

41. Paine to George Washington, 22 February 1795, re-copied by Paine in *Letter to George Washington*, 30 July 1796, *Writings*, vol. II, p. 707.

42. See Hawke, *Paine*, pp. 327-9.

43. *Agrarian Justice* (1795-6), *Writings*, vol. I, pp. 609, 605, 620. This brief

section on *Agrarian Justice* has been contributed by the editor.

44. 'To the People of England on the Invasion of England' (1804), *Writings*, vol. II, pp. 675-83.

45. See Hawke, *Paine*, pp. 343-64.

46. 'The Will of Thomas Paine', *Writings*, vol. II, pp. 1498-501.

47. Quoted in Conway, vol. II, Appendix A, p. 455.

PART TWO

4 Thomas Paine and Millenarian Radicalism

J.F.C. Harrison

It is perhaps somewhat unusual to link the name of Thomas Paine, whose image is that of the great atheist or infidel (though actually, of course, he was a deist) with a religious belief such as millenarianism.[1] However, it is not the purpose of this chapter to try to prove that Thomas Paine was a millenarian. As far as I know, he never expressed any thoughts on the subject. I am concerned with the influence of his views on his contemporaries, and would like to answer some questions as to why they were so popular with certain sections of the working people. Whether or not we accept the estimate of 200,000 copies of *Rights of Man* sold by 1793 (and the figure has been disputed), there is no doubt that it far outsold any other radical publication of the time, and became, as E.P. Thompson has said, 'one of the two foundation texts of the English working-class movement' (the other, incidentally, was a religious work, Bunyan's *Pilgrim's Progress*). Thompson has shown how Paine's influence transformed the popular radical movement from 1791-2:

> In twelve months his name became a household word. There were few places in the British Isles where his book had not penetrated. It served as a touchstone, dividing the gentlemen reformers and patrician Whigs from a minority

73

of radical manufacturers and professional men who sought an alliance with the labourers and artisans, welcomed Paine's social and economic proposals, and looked in the direction of a Republic. Pitt's long-delayed decision to prosecute Paine signalled the opening of the era of repression. The outlawry of Paine (and the banning of *Rights of Man*) was preceded and accompanied by a sustained effort by authority to meet the reformers in the field. 'As we have now got the stone to roll', Paine wrote to Walker in the summer of 1792, 'it must be kept going by cheap publications. This will embarrass the Court gentry more than anything else, because it is a ground they are not used to.'[2]

Paine's impact on the radicals was twofold: first, through his formulation of ideas of popular democracy and social reform; and second, through his deistical and anti-clerical ideas. His influence in England came mainly from the dissemination of his two works, *Rights of Man* (1791-2) and *The Age of Reason* (1794-6). This process coincided with, and was indeed (somewhat paradoxically) actually assisted by, a tradition of popular millenarianism. Let us take for instance the following specific example, which I found in the Home Office papers for 1795.[3] In May of that year the Mayor of Hastings wrote to the Home Office about a suspicious stranger who had come to the town about three weeks previously. His name was Leigh and he was 'employed generally' (when not distributing seditious handbills) 'in reading Paine's *Rights of Man*, Brothers' *Prophecies* and other books of that description.' According to a Home Office check on him, Leigh was a member of the London Corresponding Society and lived at Newington, Surrey. He was 'paid' by a Mr Fields who lived near Blackfriars Bridge, and was associated with the radical peer, Lord Stanhope.

This should alert us to the possibility of a connection. The question is, was it wholly in the minds of the authorities, or was there a link between Brothers and *Rights of Man*? Consider briefly who Richard Brothers (1757-1824) was. He appeared before the public suddenly in 1794, and attracted much attention. He was an ex-naval officer (lieutenant on half-pay) and became aware that he was the Prince of the Hebrews and Nephew of the Almighty — for his surname

'Brothers' denoted that he was descended from King David through James, one of the *brothers* of Jesus. He had visions, and also interpreted contemporary events. From the summer of 1794 to the spring of 1795, Brothers was visited daily by many people; his writings circulated all over the kingdom, and were published in America and France. Pamphlets defending and attacking him proliferated, and followers began to declare themselves. Despite denials by his followers, Brothers' writings contained opinions and prophecies which had strong political implications. 'The Lord God commands me to say to you, George the Third, King of England that immediately on my being revealed ... to the Hebrews as their Prince ... your crown must be delivered to me, that all your power and authority may instantly cease'.[4] The Lord God also commanded him to declare that the radical reformers on trial for high treason were innocent; that the war with France should be ended since the French people had 'the judgement of God in their favour'; and that in any case Britain and her allies would be defeated, in fulfilment of the prophecies in Daniel and Revelation. A glance at the Home Office papers for 1794-5 indicates the mood in government circles at this time: fear of a French invasion and the urgent need for plans to thwart it; apprehension at the spread of anti-war feeling among all ranks of society; anger against the 'treasonable' practices and views of the radical reformers and the suspected disloyalty of dissenters. Shortages of corn and high bread prices were causing concern; and there were local riots of miners in Cornwall, colliers in Leicester and 'mobs' in Newcastle and Bristol. At the opening of Parliament in October 1795 the King's coach was attacked, amidst cries of 'Bread, Peace, No Pitt'. Habeas Corpus had been temporarily suspended in May 1794, and the Seditious Meetings and Treasonable Practices Acts followed the peace demonstrations of 1795. In a climate of repression and, at times, hysteria, it was not difficult for the administration to believe that millenarian writings and prophecies might be sufficient to spark off the explosive mixture of social discontent and radical sentiment. In March 1795 Brothers was arrested and brought before the Privy Council. He was examined on suspicion of treason. But his interrogators found insufficient evidence to substantiate the charge and decided therefore to proceed on medical rather than political grounds. Evidence of madness was produced and Brothers was committed to a lunatic asylum. He continued to issue prophetic writings; but most of his followers soon transferred their allegiance to a new messiah, the prophetess Joanna Southcott.

Our next question must be: do we have any evidence that Brothers' followers were also Paineites?; were there others like Mr Leigh in Hastings? And if so, how and why was this possible? Probably a majority of Brothers' followers (and certainly a majority of Joanna Southcott's) were not politically radical. But an important minority of them were. Among the best known of these was William Sharp, the engraver and friend of William Blake. Many scholars are familiar with his engraving of Paine, after Romney's well-known portrait; but probably fewer are aware that in 1795 Sharp also engraved a portrait of Brothers, inscribed 'Richard Brothers, Prince of the Hebrews', together with the testimony: 'Fully believing this to be the Man whom GOD has appointed, I engrave his likeness.' Sharp was by this time a well-established London engraver, with an international reputation, the friend of John Flaxman, Henry Fuseli, Philip de Loutherbourg, and others in the world of artists and illustrators. He had been a radical reformer since the time of the American Revolution, and was a member of the Society for Constitutional Information when it was formed in 1780. He became a Swedenborgian in the 1780s, and possibly also a mesmerist. But from the spring of 1789 the French Revolution changed the thinking of men like Sharp. The Society for Constitutional Information (SCI), which had fallen into the doldrums, was revived early in 1791, and from March 1792 until the trials of 1794 Sharp was actively involved in it. Paine, of course, was also an honorary member of the SCI, and wished to donate the royalties from his *Rights of Man* to the society, which it had done much to revive. Sharp was in close touch with Horne Tooke, Brand Hollis, Thomas Holcroft and other republicans and Jacobin supporters. When therefore the government decided in May 1794 to move against the reformers in London it was not surprising that 'Citizen Sharp' was called before the Privy Council for examination. He tried to play down his involvement with the SCI, particularly his membership of a committee to meet with the London Corresponding Society, and in general left the impression of being something less than candid. His friends thought that he was lucky not to be indicted along with Thomas Hardy, Horne Tooke and others in the treason trials. Soon after this he declared his belief in Brothers, and from 1801 he became a leading supporter of Joanna Southcott.

Sharp's friend, William Tooke Harwood, was in a similar position. He was from Norwich (a noted centre of radical reformism) and was a captain (later colonel) of dragoons. His uncle, William Tooke of Purley, was a radically inclined business man, whose *protégé* was John Horne Tooke, an eccentric reformer and conversationalist from the days of Wilkes onwards. Harwood was a member of SCI and gave evidence on behalf of Horne Tooke when his friend was brought to trial. He was friendly with William Godwin and married Holcroft's eldest daughter in 1796. Like Sharp he was attracted to millenarianism and was shortly to appear as a follower of Joanna Southcott.

The connection between the reform societies and millenarianism, then, is not difficult to document. What we have now to explain is why this should have been so; and why admirers of *Rights of Man* could become disciples of Brothers without any apparent inconsistency. The matter will become clearer if we consider the nature of millenarian belief.

Millenarians believed that the world was to be transformed by the second coming of Christ and the establishment of the kingdom of God on earth. This state would last for a thousand years, after which would come the last judgement. During the period of the millennium the saints (that is, the Christian martyrs and all faithful Christians who have suffered) would reign with Christ. There were differences of view, however, between those Christians who believed that Christ's second coming would precede the millennium (pre-millennialists) and those who thought that the second advent would follow the millennium (post-millennialists). From these differences stemmed others. The pre-millennialists were predisposed towards the establishment of the millennium by divine, cataclysmic action, whereas the post-millennialists were prone to think that the kingdom of God would come gradually as the result of Christian, human instrumentalities. For either of these views there was ample scriptural support,

so that the choice between a revolutionary or reformist interpretation had to be made on other than theological grounds.

From these differences in interpretation and emphasis a
variety of types of millennial concern was possible, ranging
from sophisticated study of the biblical books of prophecy to
divine revelations concerning the immediate arrival of Christ
on earth. The French Revolution excited a spate of inter-
pretations on both sides of the Atlantic designed to show that
the world was entering upon the last days. Millennialism was
widely espoused by leading scholars and divines. In America
the names of Timothy Dwight (President of Yale), John H.
Livingston (President of Rutgers) and Joseph Priestley come
to mind: in Britain, George Stanley Faber, Edward King and
Edward Irving. A spate of pamphlets and sermons by Church
of England clergy and orthodox American ministers poured
forth from the 1790s; and there was constant reference back
to the prophetical studies of Sir Isaac Newton, Joseph Mede
and William Whiston.

In addition to these intellectually sophisticated millennial-
ists there were also many popular, largely self-educated
adventist millenarians. They were the people condemned by
the opulent classes as fanatics and imposters, and by historians as cranks and the lunatic fringe. The distinction between
what may be called respectable, orthodox, scholarly millennialism on the one hand, and popular (or folk) millenarianism
on the other, is useful for analytical purposes; but the division
is not hard and fast. Those who believed in the millennium
had the option of combining so many variables that a millennialist or a millenarian could be placed at any point along a
continuum of belief. Millennialism and millenarianism were
ways of looking at the world, rather than specific doctrines.
This was at the root of the difference between the millennialism of seventeenth- and eighteenth-century divines and
scholars (many of them fellows of Cambridge colleges), and
the popular millenarian tradition stemming from the radical
sects of the English Revolution. It is the tone and temper of
the popular millenarians, the way in which they used the
texts and symbols from Daniel and Revelation, which is
distinctive. They were the enthusiasts, the fanatics, the come-
outers. Their beliefs were derived from a literal, eclectic interpretation of the prophetic scriptures, and a divine revelation

vouchsafed to them directly. A simplicity, often crudity, seemed to mark their mentality, for their reliance on the supernatural enabled them to dispense with many of the limitations imposed by logic and reason. Moderation and gradualness did not commend themselves as virtues, but rather were signs of lack of faith. The basic principles of good and evil in the world were crystal clear, and life was to be lived by the light of this absolute standard, with no compromises.

The 1790s were dominated by a mood of revolutionary expectation. The events in France, coming so shortly after the American revolution, encouraged radicals and alarmed conservatives. A consciousness of living in a time of enormous change turned men's minds towards the need for some explanation. Millenarianism provided one such account. The world was now living in the last days before the coming of the millennium. The fall of European monarchies, the captivity of the pope and later the rise of Bonaparte were interpreted as fulfilling scriptural prophecies. A new heaven and a new earth were not far away. It was in this mood that Paine's *Rights of Man* and *Age of Reason* were received. 'Hey for the New Jerusalem! The Millennium! And peace and eternal beatitude be unto the soul of Thomas Paine', wrote Thomas Holcroft, the dramatist, to William Godwin.[5]

Apart from personal friendships and common membership of the reform societies, there were also more intellectually substantial arguments for associating millenarianism with radicalism. To the millenarian who identified the Church of Rome with Anti-Christ, the French attack on Catholicism could only be welcomed. It was evidence that the last days were nigh, and the French revolutionaries were the agents of Providence in fulfilling the prophecies. For radical reformers the events in France similarly confirmed the democratic and republican principles they had held since the time of the American Revolution. There was room here for some overlap with the millenarian position, despite the religious infidelity (usually deism) of popular radicalism. It was this which alarmed William Hamilton Reid, an ex-radical, into denouncing the 'Mystics, Muggletonians, Millennaries' as auxiliaries of infidelity. He instanced popular speakers in Spitalfields, where 'the French system of politics insensibly attached itself to the auxiliary ideas of prophecies fulfilling on the Continent'; and gave details of a circle of 'infidel mystics' at Hoxton, known as the Ancient Deists, which he alleged was composed of 'alchemists, astrologers, calculators, mystics, magnetizers, prophets and projectors of every class'.[6] Reid wrote of a 'Millennium of Infidelity', and was disgusted with the inconsistency of 'infidels' who attended Christian worship. Yet he well knew that dissenting Christians (including millenarians) who believed in 'the sufficiency of the spirit's teaching' were, in some respects, not far removed from the position of Thomas Paine. In the first part of *Age of Reason*, Paine declared, 'My own mind is my own church'; and admitted that revelation from God might have a personal (but not general) validity. It is possible therefore, following Reid, to see in the popular radicalism of the mid-1790s a sort of synthesis of Christian and infidel millenarianism. In the case of individuals such as Sharp, however, it is not easy to distinguish the various elements or types of millenarianism at any one time. It is tempting to look for a progression from a radical–political millenarianism to a religious, non-political millenarianism, or vice versa. But on close examination this breaks down. Sharp had been a Radical since the days of the American Revolutionary War and was a Swedenborgian in the 1780s. His involvement with the radical reformers of the 1790s and with Brothers appears to be a continuation of his earlier interests, and he was later to transfer his allegiance to Joanna Southcott. Political radicalism and religious millenarianism were not alternatives so much as different aspects of the same phenomenon. From the personal angle, millenarianism has to be seen, not as a progression, but as a generalised belief about the world and the changes going on in it, which could be expressed in varying modes at different times, but which remained a constant for the individual concerned.

Paine's religion was the deism of the Enlightenment. He coupled this with humanism and started a Society of Theophilanthropists, the object of which was (quoting Samuel Adams), 'to renovate the age by inculcating in the minds of youth the fear and love of the Deity and universal philanthropy'.[7] Theologically, Paine was quite conservative — despite the furore occasioned by his biblical criticism in Part II of *The Age of Reason*. He wrote the first part of *The Age of*

Reason to assert 'true' as opposed to 'fabulous' theology, and to warn the French people against rushing into atheism. His arguments to prove the existence of God were in the main-stream of natural theology: 'the creation is of itself demon-stration of the existence of a Creator ... When we see a watch, we have a positive evidence of the existence of a watchmaker, as if we saw him.' William Paley himself could not have done better. Paine's great contribution was not that his theology was original, but that he reached out to artisans and labouring people and linked theological with political radicalism. He was able to do this because of a long tradition of popular religious dissent, which was strongly anti-clerical and which in certain forms shaded off into deism and free-thinking Christianity. Millenarianism was sometimes, though not always, an ingredient in this popular dissent.

Basically millenarianism was an ideology of change. It focused attention on the great changes which were currently taking place in these last days, and promised a vast trans-formation of the social order when all things would be made new. Men and women who were looking eagerly for a new heaven and a new earth could not but be consciously aware that the future would be utterly different from the present, and their thinking thus became attuned to the idea of change. This in itself was an achievement: it was the beginning of 'a new dawn of social consciousness'. For the most part this social change was in a radical direction. In a society dominated by an aristocratic and Anglican establishment, any movement outside its paternalistic control was a radical departure, a potential threat to that deference, respect and subordination which was held to be necessary for social stability. The very existence of ideas and voluntary associations independent of traditional institutions and leaders was suspect. All millenar-ians were liable to find themselves regarded as radicals, simply because they were dissident. For some millenarians, as we have seen, the charge had more substance. The links between some of Brothers' followers and political radicalism in the 1790s could be further strengthened. For instance, the printers and publishers of radical tracts frequently performed the same service for the millenarians. Brothers' publisher, George Riebau, was a member of the London Corresponding Society. H.D. Symonds, Arthur Seale and B. Crosby were other radicals who published Brothers' and Joanna's works along with Paine, Spence and Volney.

I have not found any evidence that Paine was personally acquainted with Brothers. Given Paine's general criticism of biblical prophecy and revealed religion it seems unlikely that he would have approved of the 'Nephew of the Almighty'. However, Paine and Brothers were perhaps not quite as far apart as may at first be supposed. Our neat categorisations should be used only with caution. We need to be aware always of the sensibilities of an age. Take, for instance, Paine's essay on the *Origins of Freemasonry*, written in New York in 1805 and published posthumously in 1810. It might be expected that Paine, with his condemnation of what he regarded as ignorance, superstition and mummery would have little time for freemasonry. The masons' secrecy and ceremonies would surely be ridiculed. Not a bit of it. Paine writes understandingly of the masons and contrasts masonry favourably with Christianity. He is convinced that masons are the descendants of the ancient Druids: 'Masonry is derived and is the remains of the religion of the ancient Druids . . . who, by all accounts . . . were a wise, learned and moral class of men.'[8] Brothers' British Israelism and his claim to be the Prince of the Hebrews is part of this same school of speculative mythology.

The 'invisible' Hebrews, who he was to lead back to the Holy Land, were accounted for by Brothers in two ways. First were the descendants of those Israelites who had been carried into captivity at various times by the Assyrians, together with some who had travelled freely into foreign lands. Secondly, some Jews had been converted to Christianity by Jesus and the apostles. They had been persecuted, taken to Rome, sold into slavery and dispersed throughout Europe. In remote times many of these exiles had found their way to Britain. Hence a large part of the present British population was of Hebrew extraction, and Brothers had no difficulty in assigning his friends and supporters to one or other of the ten lost tribes of Israel. He himself, of course, was of the kingly house of David. Fanciful as this theory may sound, it was no less credible than other contemporary speculations such as are found in Blake's *Jerusalem*.

The pedigree of these ideas is to be traced in the writings of the speculative mythologists, whose antiquarian discoveries provided a slender basis for a highly romantic view of the early history of Britain. It was claimed that England was the seat of antediluvian religion, and even that the Garden of Eden was situated in the British Isles. The patriarchal religion of Abraham was preserved among the Druid priesthood. 'Adam was a Druid, and Noah', wrote Blake. The ground for these claims lay in an euthemerist view of mythology, which regarded myth not as an explanation of some mysterious phenomenon of nature but as history presented in a special (sometimes distorted and obscure) way.

In the context of this intellectual milieu, Brothers' theories of British Israelism do not appear unusually far-fetched; and there is evidence that both he and some of his followers were interested in antiquarian and mythological researches. But it is not relevant to pursue this matter further at present. Our purpose is to suggest that the new sensibility to millenarianism in the 1790s and early 1800s may be related to the same intellectual currents and social impulses as account for the popularity of speculative mythology. From snatches of evidence such as the essay on the *Origins of Freemasonry* it would seem that Paine was closer to the intellectual world of Brothers and Sharp than is sometimes realised.

In the years following Paine's death, the same pattern of a connection between infidelity and millenarianism was repeated. At the Hopkins Street chapel in London the Rev. Erasmus Perkins (alias George Cannon) and Robert Wedderburn (a Jamaican tailor) preached a mixture of Paineite radicalism and millenarian expectation; their writings reveal a strange combination of working-class Unitarianism, eighteenth-century Deism and plebeian chiliasm. Richard Carlile, who republished Paine's works, was at the centre of a radical movement based on the Rotunda which connected with the millenarians who followed Zion Ward. By the 1830s and 1840s, millenarian and radical beliefs frequently overlapped. If we dig into the history of popular radicalism almost anywhere before 1850, the chances are good that we shall unearth millenarian as well as Paineite references. The Owenites in the 1830s drew heavily upon millenarian ideas and vocabulary; and early historians of socialism compared the utopian socialists with millenarian sects.

If we find this connection strange it is probably because of our assumption that religious and secular cultures were, or ought to have been, rigidly separated. This is an anachronism. For many working people there was no incompatibility between the two; life has to be lived whole, not compartmentalised. Belief systems are constructed out of practical needs, not a regard for logic.

Nevertheless, at the end of the day we are left with something of a paradox. We have argued that the enthusiastic reception of Paine's ideas is to be explained in part by the way in which they harmonised with a mood of millenarian hope and expectation. Paine himself was conscious of living in an era of unprecedented change: 'We have it in our power', he wrote in *Common Sense*, 'to begin the world over again. A situation, similar to the present, hath not happened since the days of Noah until now. The birthday of a new world is at hand'.[9] That most interesting of all the millenarians of the late eighteenth century, William Blake, repudiated Paine's deism. But after reading Bishop Watson's *An Apology for the Bible* (in reply to *The Age of Reason*), Blake concluded: 'It appears to me now that Tom Paine is a better Christian than the Bishop.'[10] In Blake's view Paine had been 'sent' to attack, not Christianity, but its perversions by scholars and priests. Today deism utterly fails to arouse the fear and opposition that it did in orthodox Christians of the early nineteenth century. Paine's confession in *The Age of Reason* —

> I believe in one God, and no more; and I hope for happiness beyond this life.
> I believe in the equality of man; and I believe that religious duties consist in doing justice, loving mercy, and endeavoring to make our fellow creatures happy.[11]

— appears as unexceptionable to a majority of our fellow citizens. Too much of our history is written from the angle of the successful and the orthodox. Thomas Paine related to a different tradition. Perhaps his overlap with millenarian radicalism is part of the history of a great area of popular and unorthodox religion which has still to be written.

Notes

1. For millenarianism in this period see J.F.C. Harrison, *The Second Coming: Popular Millenarianism, 1780-1850* (London: Routledge and Kegan Paul, 1979).

2. E.P. Thompson, *The Making of the English Working Class* (London: Gollancz, 1963), p. 111.

3. Home Office Papers, PRO, HO 42/34 (letter from Edward Milward, Jr, to Duke of Portland, 1 May 1795).

4. Richard Brothers, *A Revealed Knowledge*, Book II, in *The World's Doom; or the Cabinet of Fate Unlocked*, 2 vols (London: B. Crosby, 1795), vol. I, p. 353.

5. James K. Hopkins, *A Woman to Deliver her People* (Austin: University of Texas Press, 1982), p. 157.

6. William Hamilton Reid, *The Rise and Dissolution of the Infidel Societies in this Metropolis* (London, J. Hatchard, 1800), pp. 14, 91, repr. in V.E. Neubury (ed.), *Literacy and Society* (London: Woburn Press, 1971).

7. Edward Royle, *Victorian Infidels* (Manchester: Manchester University Press, 1974), pp. 27-8.

8. Thomas Paine, *An Essay on the Origin of Freemasonry* (London: R. Carlile, 1818), p. 5.

9. Thomas Paine, *Common Sense* (London: R. Carlile, 1819), p. 49.

10. William Blake, *Poetry and Prose*, ed. Geoffrey Keynes (London: Nonesuch Press, 1967), p. 767.

11. Thomas Paine, *The Age of Reason*, Part I (London: R. Carlile, 1818), p. 3.

5 Debts and Liabilities:
William Cobbett and Thomas Paine

Ian Dyck

I have never made it a consideration of whether the subject
was popular or unpopular, but whether it was right or
wrong.

Paine, Crisis X (March 1782)

Twenty years experience has taught me, that people will
read that which is written to their taste, and that sooner or
later, reason and truth will prevail, if they are put before
sensible people in a way to be clearly understood.

Cobbett to Matthew Carey (16 July 1815)

For someone who would invent the periodical radical press,
and in the process create a new populist radicalism for the
English working class, William Cobbett was surprisingly
short of intellectual debts. The first and most important
explanation is that his success in the popular press, as well as
his motivation as a Radical, derived not from books or from
political mentors, but from an assortment of first-hand
experiences with the hardships of English rural workers.[1] His
second major debt dated back to his youth in rural Surrey,
where he lived and worked with country people, himself 'a
sort of labourer'.[2] As a boy he scared birds and as a youth he
held plough — the two statutory rites of passage in farm

labouring life. Field work, country fairs and popular legends were formative of Cobbett's character and world-view; they endowed him with a unique ability to communicate with country folk, even on subjects as wide-ranging as economics, politics, agriculture, morality and history.

Cobbett sought to radicalise the English worker, but he also endeavoured to cultivate and defend a world-view defined by nature, landscape, tradition, and by oral rather than printed culture. Books and newspapers, he often remarked, were not the only avenue to learning; nor were they essential to the acquisition of radical political ideas. Not the popular press but the plain experience of suffering, in his view, was the primary architect of popular radicalism. It was Cobbett's understanding that the oral culture of rural England was evolving its own language of protest during the late eighteenth and early nineteenth centuries. The task of his *Political Register*, therefore, was to transmit to the labourers, via the pedlar's pack, a prose rendition of experiences and ideologies already current in the popular mind.[3]

No other contemporary Radical would join Cobbett in styling his ideas and methods upon popular rural culture — not Francis Place, not Henry Hunt, not Francis Burdett, not Richard Carlile, not even Thomas Paine. None of these leaders were agrarian-oriented in their language or their politics; and none shared Cobbett's willingness to identify with the oral traditions of the rural world. Cobbett was therefore unique among Radicals, and he defended this uniqueness by quarrelling successively with Place, Burdett, Hunt and Carlile. Only Paine, of the major radical thinkers, would Cobbett identify as a positive contributor to the radical movement; as he poetically phrased it, 'At [Paine's] expiring flambeau, I lighted my taper.'[4] For Cobbett — a great egoist — this was uncharacteristically charitable; but from a cultural and religious perspective, his declared indebtedness to Paine was manifestly distorted and untrue.

Like innumerable other Englishmen, Cobbett first encountered radical ideas in *Rights of Man*. As a young soldier recently returned from New Brunswick, he found solace in Paine's support for the common soldier. The doctrines of liberty and equality also sounded promising, especially in the wake of Cobbett's discovery of the appropriation of a part of his fellow soldiers' pay by the officers of his regiment.[5] In a condition 'brim full of republicanism',[6] and doubtless mindful of Paine's declaration that soldiers 'might be said to be without a friend',[7] he composed his first tract — an anonymous pamphlet entitled 'The Soldier's Friend' (1792). 'Let it be considered', he later apologised,

> that I had just arrived in England; that I was a perfect novice in politics, never having, to my recollection, read even a newspaper while abroad; and, let it be considered, too, that I took up the book of Paine (just then published) with my mind full of indignation at the abuses which I myself had witnessed [in the army].[8]

Not for long was Cobbett a disciple of Paine. In 1794, after taking ideological refuge in Pennsylvania, he became saddled with guilt over his previous hostility towards the British establishment. His native country was already at war with republican France, and perhaps soon to be at war with America itself. Britian needed an anti-Jacobin voice in America, someone to answer the critics of British conventions and institutions.[9]

'Peter Porcupine' (as Cobbett called himself, though Paine preferred to call him 'Peter Skunk'),[10] was undaunted by the task. As an anti-Jacobin pamphleteer he poured unlimited energy into his private war against republicanism and democracy. Joseph Priestley, Benjamin Franklin and Thomas Jefferson were crudely lambasted in his pamphlets and periodicals, but his sharpest words were always reserved for Paine:

> Whenever or wherever he breathes his last, he will excite neither sorrow nor compassion; no friendly hand will close his eyes, not a groan will be uttered, not a tear will be shed. Like *Judas* he will be remembered by posterity; men will learn to express all that is base, malignant, treacherous, unnatural and blasphemous, by the single monosyllable, Paine.[11]

The prophecy would indeed come to pass, but ironically it was none other than Cobbett who would later excavate the very bones that he now wished into everlasting obscurity.

For ten long years Cobbett maligned Paine as 'an unconscionable dog', a 'wretched traitor and apostate', and 'a man famous for nothing but his blasphemy and his hatred of England'.[12] No epithet was too misleading or vile; after all, Cobbett held Paine personally responsible for defiling him (and other common Englishmen) of his political innocence and native patriotism. Then suddenly, in 1803, Cobbett fell comparatively quiet on the subject of Paine, and from then until 1809, he diverted his wrath towards the ruling class of Regency England.

It was Cobbett's intention, upon returning to England in 1800, to resume his campaign against Paine and the Jacobins.[13] But the war was short-lived, for as he rediscovered rural England, and as he re-entered the English cottage, he found that the plenty and contentment of his youth had been replaced by hunger, misery and pauperism.[14] In Cobbett this experience generated an emotional and political crisis, for his anti-Jacobinism had in part been inspired by an understanding that the labourers of monarchical England were materially better off than their republican brethren in the United States. Suddenly he had to come to terms with this deception:

> I myself, in the early part of my writing life was deceived ...; but, when, in [1804], I revisited the English labourer's dwelling, and that, too, after having so recently witnessed the happiness of labourers in America; when I saw that the *clock* was gone; that even the *Sunday-coat* was gone; when I saw those whom I had known the most neat, cheerful and happy beings on earth, and these my own countrymen too, had become the most wretched and forlorn of human beings, I looked seriously and inquired patiently into the matter; and this inquiry into the causes of an effect which had so deep an impression on my mind, led to that series of exertions, which have *occupied my whole life, since that time, to better the lot of the Labourers.*[15]

Immediately Cobbett put his anti-Jacobinism onto hold, and in the *Political Register* he assumed the task of exposing the principles, the persons and the institutions which had so greatly reduced the circumstances of the country workers. But the task was not easy, for Cobbett had no experience in analysing the origin of poverty and oppression. High politics, conservative rhetoric and wartime diplomacy had for so long dominated his journalistic themes that he lapsed temporarily into ideological confusion.

Two obvious causes of the labourer's impoverishment — increased indirect taxation and corruptions in the Poor Law — were the doings of Parliament, hence it was to Westminster that Cobbett eventually turned. He began to agitate for a moderate reform of the House of Commons, but his focus was upon the election of uncorruptible candidates (such as himself) rather than upon a specific plan for political and economic reform. Of course he was familiar with the writings of Paine, but it was a decade or more since he had last picked them up, and his sole object had then been to subject them to an anti-Jacobin critique.

It was not until Cobbett was gaoled in Newgate (1810-12) for seditious libel[16] that he re-examined the writings of Paine. The first text he studied was *The Decline and Fall of the English System of Finance* in which Paine prophesied the demise of 'the thing' (to use Cobbett's phrase) — that unholy network of sinecures, patronage, national debts, paper money and the 'funding system'. Immediately Cobbett converted to Paineite economics.[17] Earlier in America he had maligned the *Decline and Fall*, but now it offered what Cobbett was looking for — a convincing and radical explanation of the causes of inflation, low farm wages, high taxation and a rising national debt.[18]

Although Cobbett followed his own course of radical development, it is tempting to suggest that he was destined to a *rapprochement* with Paine. Both men, after all, were founding fathers of radical working class politics; both began their writing careers by defending their modest occupations against a rapacious ruling class; both became critics of high finance and paper currency; both were masters of popular prose; both were hostile towards the 'learned languages'; and both nurtured the concept of the welfare state. Nevertheless, enormous divisions remained, even after Cobbett's re-birth as a Radical: Paine was a republican, a deist and a daring free-thinker; Cobbett remained a monarchist, a Trinitarian and a conservative moralist. Paine drank spirits to excess; Cobbett drank only beer and water; Paine (though of Quaker stock) was slack and untidy in his work habits; Cobbett was well-organized and puritanical; Paine welcomed the new industrial civilisation; Cobbett wanted a return to the agrarian simplicity of 'old England'.

Cobbett was not unaware of these differences. He also knew the legal risks attached to public defences of the name and memory of Paine. But in the 1810s, with the radical movement virtually terminated by the wartime Tory ministries, and with the circulation of the *Political Register* in sharp decline, Cobbett gambled that the name of Paine might serve as a touchstone for a radical renewal. The plan backfired. Among the readers who could afford the one shilling cover-price of the stamped *Register*, Paine and his legacy were a greater liability than ever. Cobbett's readership dwindled further, but in 1816, by a stroke of populist ingenuity, he rescued himself from impending oblivion. The post-war suffering of the people made them a captive audience for a new political literature. After circumventing the stamp laws, Cobbett launched a periodical broadside, price two-pence, which was carried in the pedlar's pack to the cottages, street-corners and fields of England.[19]

Cobbett, no less than the magistrates, was astonished by the success of his new venture.[20] The ruling class had seen nothing like it since the days of the cheap edition of the *Rights of Man*. But at least *that* publication, they must have reasoned, was a one-time thing, whereas Cobbett's sheets appeared week after week in the pubs, the cottages and the workshops. Moreover, Cobbett approached the people more directly and more intimately than had Paine. He illuminated precise faces in the crowd; he named and embarrassed specific adversaries of the labouring man; above all he made sensational appeals to the affronted dignity and intelligence of working people. 'Friends and Fellow Countrymen', he began an early two-penny *Register*,

Whatever the pride of rank, of riches, or of scholarship may have induced some men to believe, or to affect to believe the real strength and all the resources of a country, ever have sprung, and ever must spring, from the labour of its people ...

Cobbett here joined Paine in proclaiming the economic importance of the labouring man. But where Paine would have gone on to detail his own private plan of democratic reform, Cobbett injected his proclamation into the hearts and minds of his readers, while assuring them that they already knew their own worth, and that they themselves were managers of a defensive campaign to humanise and reform the governing classes. He continued:

> With this correct idea of your own worth in your minds, with what indignation must you hear yourselves called the Populace, the Rabble, the Mob, the Swinish Multitude, ... Shall we *never* see the day when these men change their tone! Will they never cease to look upon you as brutes! I trust they will change their tone, and that the day of the change is at no great distance![21]

Paine's styles and methods were not these. His was an offensive rather than defensive strategy; he did not want to reform the ruling class but to get rid of it. Nor did he seek a radical base in the popular will; always he led from the front, carving out a new way rather than spring-cleaning the old.

In the early months of the two-penny *Register*, Cobbett seldom invoked the name and legacy of Paine. Instead he operated within a new radical context which distilled from popular culture the grievances of the common people. It was a radical form co-created by Cobbett and the labourers of England. The *Register* used the language of the people to guide them towards an ideology that was economically radical (thanks to Paine's influence), politically moderate and culturally conservative. More than Paine, Cobbett was given to minute topical enquiry into the human consequences of class tyranny and political corruption, and less than Paine he was concerned with detailing the infrastructure of the democratic state. The Enlightenment jargon of the *Rights of Man* was seldom to be found in the cheap *Register*; instead Cobbett appealed to the old English virtues of justice and fair play.

Rather than follow Paine's lead of using the language of the *philosophes* and of the American revolutionaries, he simply ventilated the peoples' indignation against 'the insolent men, who call us the *"Lower Orders"*', and who refer to the 'Poor' as if to suggest that working people belong to poverty: 'I, in behalf of the labourers, reject this appellation with scorn.'[22]

Populism came naturally to Cobbett. He did not contrive his way to eye-level with the agricultural masses. His frequent use of the first person, and of 'us', 'them' and 'we', was the honest language of cultural identity, not of artful condescension. 'I say WE', he once remarked, 'because I never do and I never can separate myself ... from the Labouring Classes.'[23] This was a commitment that Paine did not feel or want. A close mental and cultural affinity with the traditions of the English common people would have cramped his aspiration for intellectual freedom and cultural exploration. Misplaced sentiment towards popular inclinations might sap revolutionary strength and potential. 'We have it in our power to begin the world over again',[24] said Paine, but that power was often tenuous and ephemeral. Achievement of the new beginning, in his view, always required absolute loyalty to enlightened and systematic progress within every sphere of the human experience.

The labouring people of England were reformers, but they had preoccupations, most notably a propensity to look backward as much as forward. The 'golden age' and 'merrie England' formed one of the great themes of English ballads and protest songs during the late eighteenth and early nineteenth centuries. The English workers — both artisans and farm labourers — clung to a belief, transmitted by oral culture, that the worker had materially and emotionally prospered, not only in the distant past, but during the first two-thirds of the eighteenth century:

> Our venerable father remembers the year
> When a man could earn three shillings a day and his beer
> He then could live well, keep his family neat,
> But now he must work for eight shillings a week.[25]

Song after song reiterated the message:

In former times, our fathers say,
The times were different far from now
The taxes were not half so high,
The poor man kept a pig and a cow[26]

Cobbett shared in this popular understanding of the past. To his mind, not only songs but physical artefacts confirmed the historical sensibilities of the poor:

Everything of tradition; all the old sayings of the country, which come down from father to son, show, that England was, in all former times, a country singularly happy; that its people were better off than those of any other country known to it. The words '*English hospitality*', had not their origin in nothing. The capaciousness of the cellars in ancient houses; the capaciousness of the kitchens; the old songs, whenever they treat or allude to matters of this sort, all show that good living was a great characteristic of the nation.[27]

As a man of the people, Cobbett was always careful to align his economic enquiry with the traditions and experiences of the poor. Paine, on the other hand, though decrying the hardship created by taxation and inflation, proceeded immediately to his arguments without direct reference to the experiences and testimony of the people. His radical economics therefore, were less meaningful (and less digestible) to the common man.

Cobbett's many enquiries into 'old England' were not crafty devices to enrol more readers; they were intended to reassure himself, no less than the labourers, that reform need not conflict with continuity and tradition. Paine, of course, did not seek refuge in the mystical garb of 'merrie England'. More intellectually progressive than Cobbett, and more confident in the ability of the people to grasp the abstract concept, he demanded a final break with conservatism in its every form. Anything less, he believed, was in the shadow of Edmund Burke.

In culture and religion Cobbett moved more gently than Paine. Even in economics and politics — his most radical suits — he proceeded with discretion and caution, advancing his programme only after he had established his credibility as one who knew and felt the importance of the working man, and as one who perceived popular culture from the inside. Carefully holding the labourer's trust, he freed an arm to open the door to a radical reform programme, all the while reinforcing his labourer identity with ruralist imagery and emotive references to the desperate circumstances of the cottage.

Hence despite the extensive similarities between their reform programmes, Paine and Cobbett were differently perceived by the common reader. Paine seemed to the people more seditious and revolutionary. Cobbett, on the other hand, disguised his 'sedition' by speaking the idiom of the masses. As the young James Watson (then a farm worker) recalled:

> I remember my mother being in the habit of reading Cobbett's *Register*, and saying she wondered people spoke so much against it; she saw nothing bad in it, but she saw a great many good things in it. After hearing it read ... I was of my mother's opinion.[28]

Cobbett's radicalism would flourish because it was seen to contain 'nothing bad' and nothing essentially new. At the same time as his *Register* was calling for universal suffrage, and for Paineite economic reform, his other writings called the workers' attention to other fields of human endeavour, urging them to find happiness within their given social station. His *Sermons*, for example, codified the conservative ethics of working Englishmen; his *Cottage Economy* was a manual of peasant self-help; and his *Advice to Young Men* was welcomed, even by the establishment, as an impeccable moral code for all humanity. Paine, however, enjoyed no establishment approval. His radicalism was all-encompassing; and unlike Cobbett, he neither sought nor obtained an intellectual or cultural guise for his programme of democratic revolution.

For 30 years after 1792 the politics and character of Paine was the subject of anathemas in the establishment-controlled side of the popular press.[29] 'Every individual labourer or artizan', lamented Cobbett, 'has had [an anti-Paineite] to speak to him', with the almost inevitable consequence that the people were no longer free agents in deciding upon Paine's merits and demerits:

> The active men of the present day; the fathers of families of this our day, were brought up in their youth to detest and despise his name. The boys and girls of twenty years ago were led on by the clergy and other persons in authority to burn him in effigy; a ceremony which was omitted in scarcely any one village in this whole kingdom. To burn a Tom Paine was much more popular than to burn a Guy Fawkes; whose place Paine supplied for several years on the annual festival of riotous loyalty.[30]

Because of his sympathy for popular culture, Cobbett was not prepared to give the establishment a free hand to ply the people with 'safe books' and unanswered anti-Paine ditties. In the face of his own continuing reservations about Paine's religion, he resolved to sanitise popular culture of its anti-Paine component. Then, he trusted, the people could better appreciate Paine's economics and his contribution to the founding of the cheap radical press.

The rehabilitation programme was not formally launched until Cobbett, in fear of the Power of Imprisonment Act of 1817, had safely removed himself to America, out of reach of the Attorney-General and the Home Office. There, angry and disillusioned about the long-term prospects for the reform movement, he began to compare his own exile and persecution with that of the author of the *Rights Of Man*. Paine, he now confessed, was the first person to awaken a 'spirit of enquiry' among the masses. *Rights of Man* was suppressed, to be sure, but in the minds of the people the 'spirit of enquiry' remained, later to be rekindled by the two-penny *Register*.[31] To commemmorate this liaison, Cobbett proposed to write a redemptive biography of Paine and to issue a new edition of his works.[32] Feeling that this was insufficient apology for his former onslaughts against Paine's character, he stole, in the dead of night, late in September of 1819, to Paine's farm at New Rochelle. There, shovel in hand, he reverently disinterred the very 'carcass' that he had once predestined to infamy and divine punishment.[33]

The political purpose of this morbid exercise was to give

new life to the English reformers. The bones, too, might serve as a talisman for warding off the magistrates and courts of England; the people would rally around Cobbett, if only to safeguard the sanctity of Paine's corpse. But it was not to be; the people were ill-disposed towards any effort to resurrect the memory of Paine. Cobbett's 'bone' rallies in the Midlands and London were poorly attended; nor was there an enthusiastic response to the *Register's* appeal for a public subscription to fund a Paine monument.[34] Quietly, though with remorse, Cobbett slid the bones beneath his bed.[35] But even that did not preserve him from the mockery of the radical and conservative press. Fun was everywhere poked at his venture, and all that Cobbett could muster by way of reply was a faint-hearted allusion to Paine as a man of 'distinguished talent' who in due course would be redeemed by the '*healing* hand of *time*'.[36]

The bones fiasco was the first and last great compromise of Cobbett's populism. His proximity to Paine had cost him dearly, but fortunately his losses — in terms of readership and popularity — were temporary. In short order he was able to redeem himself by taking up the cause of Queen Caroline, but the challenge presented by Paine's legacy continued to haunt him; and when restored in popular favour, he took a hard and close look at the people's understanding of the infamous Paine.

Cobbett had gambled that the English worker was prepared to distinguish between Paine's economics and religion. There lay his great mistake, for more than Cobbett appreciated, the parish priests and the 'religious' tracts had alerted the people to Paine's religious heresies. Like Paine and Cobbett, the people were anti-clerical, but they did not doubt the Trinity or the Bible as the word of God. A re-examination of *The Age of Reason* revealed to Cobbett the unpopular dimension of Paine's theology; so partly to straighten the record he composed his own religious tracts for the people, there asserting an orthodox, scripturally-based code of Christian theology and morality.[37] Even this failed to appease his critics within the ruling class. Thus in 1826, when the clerical and political establishment, in fear of electoral success by Cobbett

at a Preston by-election, questioned his own religious ortho-
doxy, he published a broadsheet in which he expressly
condemned Paine for having 'imbibed an unhappy perverse-
ness on the score of religion'. Paine was not an atheist, unlike
Richard Carlile, observed Cobbett, but nevertheless he made
a 'great error' when he 'denied the Divinity of Our Saviour'.
Therefore, Cobbett concluded, 'I now express *my decided
disapprobation of his writing, on the subject of religion*. I praise
only his writings on taxation and paper, liberty and political
science.'[38]

The 'disapprobation' was not feigned for electoral advantage. At times, however, Cobbett appeared to occupy mutual
territory with Paine on religious matters. At one point, when
disillusioned with the political righteousness and the dubious
morality of some of the clergy, he contended that 'Religion is
not an abstract idea. It is not something metaphysical. It is to
produce effect upon men's conduct, or it is good for
nothing.'[39] On the surface this approximates Paine's celebrated assertion that 'to do good is my religion', but for
Cobbett, as for the people, there was more to Christianity
than instruction in doing good. After a commitment to
charity was elicited by religion, there remained spiritual
obligations to a life of faith, sacramentalism and to public
worship of Jesus as the Son of God. Further, Cobbett and the
people would have disassociated themselves from Paine's
concept that 'My own mind is my own Church.'[40] Clerical
secular authority troubled Cobbett, and to that extent he was
prepared publicly to defend *The Age of Reason*, but that did not
cause him to abandon Christian conventions, or to resign his
commitment to the Church as an institution to unite all
Englishmen, rich as well as poor.

Cobbett appreciated that religion was not the only impedi-
ment to a rehabilitation of Paine in the popular mind. Republicanism itself was unacceptable to most Englishmen.
Whereas Cobbett and the people were prepared to criticise
individual monarchs, especially George IV, they revered the
institution of monarchy. It was Cobbett's belief, and his
transatlantic experience, that the form of government had
little influence upon the standard of living of ordinary people.
His historical studies, too, failed to confirm a necessary
relationship between popular oppression and 'the expenses or

the prerogatives of the Crown'.[41] The people agreed; they further agreed that a king, 'not under the beck of the aristocracy', working cheek-by-jowl with a democratically elected House of Commons, was the style of government best suited to the happiness and prosperity of the English.[42] The republicanism of Paine was therefore an unnecessary political wager; even worse it was a betrayal of the Constitution which for centuries had served the British well.   234787.

Above all, it was Paine's world citizenship that lost him followers among the people.[43] His country was the world, not England, and to the popular mind this was nothing less than cultural and political treason. In the heady days of the French Revolution many English workers were sympathetic towards Paine's international loyalties, but he alienated whatever was left of this opinion in 1804 when he publicly encouraged Napoleon to undertake his planned invasion of England.[44] Cobbett, meanwhile, was penning a pamphlet exhorting the English to take up arms against the prospective invaders, which pamphlet was ordered by the government to be read from every pulpit in the kingdom.[45] Of course, Cobbett was still in his Tory career, but as a Radical, too, he resisted all foreign interference in British affairs, and by military means if necessary.

In Cobbett the people of England had a life-long celebrant of Englishness — an archetypal John Bull who campaigned for bread, bacon and beer instead of the 'un-English' innovations of deism and republicanism. All 'decent' people, suggested Cobbett, love their own country first; they abhor the 'immoral and vile' sentiment of Benjamin Franklin that 'where liberty is, there is my country'.[46] Here, as often, Cobbett was taking his cue from the English labourers; but as a social journalist, too, he put Britain first. 'I am no citizen of the world', he boasted,

It is quite enough for me to think about what is best for England, Ireland and Scotland. I do not like those whose philanthropy is so enlarged as to look, as Rousseau said, to Tartary for objects of affection and commiseration, while their own countrymen are starving, or existing, on seaweed and nettles.[47]

It was a deep-seated love of England as his native land — a disposition to 'share in all her glory and in all her disgrace' — that prevented Cobbett from assuming world citizenship. There was much about America that he liked, especially its political simplicity, its economics and its happy working class, but no foreign country would he suffer to push England around with impunity. 'I wish Americans all the happiness that men can enjoy in this world', he proclaimed, 'but a nation may be a very happy without being permitted to swagger about and be saucy to England.'[48]

Doubtless, Cobbett's anti-Gallicanism and anti-Americanism were not as pronounced as the people would have liked, but never could anyone (then or now) question the sincerity and intensity of his Englishness. As a proud Englishman he tapped popular culture of past and present, while embodying in himself a prototype of old England that continues to win him admirers among Anglophiles the world over. Paine, though vastly more important than Cobbett as a world political thinker, continues to be exiled by the narrow pride of national cultures.

Karl Marx once identified Cobbett as 'a plebeian by instinct and by sympathy'.[49] The same could be said of Paine, but in his writings he chose only partly to cultivate his plebeian intuitions. As a radical writer he was steadfastly intellectual, despite his innovations in style and language; he opted to forego a Cobbett-like populism for the rationalism, deism and world citizenship of the Enlightenment. For a brief period in the 1790s, Cobbett and the working people lent consideration to these propositions. But in the long term, Cobbett and the working people preferred a reform programme made in England, for Englishmen. The ruling class (and sometimes Cobbett himself) would liken the *Political Register* to the *Rights of Man* and to *The Age of Reason*, but they were not looking beyond economics to the religion and culture of the people. As a reward for his cultural loyalty, Cobbett was licensed by the common reader to communicate a non-traditional, even Paine-influenced, reform programme. Paine, without such licence, sadly fell from grace in the popular mind.

Notes

1. Ian Dyck, 'William Cobbett and the Farm Workers, 1790-1835' (Unpublished DPhil Thesis, University of Sussex, 1986), esp. ch. 2.

2. *Political Register* (hereafter PR), 30 August 1834, pp. 529-30.

3. Dyck, 'William Cobbett', chs 5-6.

4. PR, 18 December 1819, p. 472.

5. PR, 17 June 1809, pp. 899-915; *Life and Adventures of Peter Porcupine*, ed. G.D.H. Cole (London: Nonesuch Press, 1927), pp. 32-7. See George Spater, *William Cobbett: The Poor Man's Friend* (London: Cambridge University Press, 1982), pp. 30-6.

6. *Porcupine's Gazette*, 12 August 1799, quoted in Mary Clark, *Peter Porcupine in America* (1937) (New York: Beekham reprint, 1974), p. 8. See also PR, 17 June 1809, p. 903.

7. Paine, *Rights of Man* (1791-2), ed. Henry Collins (Harmondsworth: Penguin, 1969), p. 290.

8. PR, 5 October 1805, pp. 522-3.

9. See *Life and Adventures*, pp. 86-7; *The Rush-Light*, no. VI (30 August 1800); PR, 29 September 1804, pp. 450-1; *Porcupine's Works* (London, 1801), vol. V, p. 169, vol. IX, p. 246.

10. Paine and Cobbett never met face to face, but for Paine's allusion to Cobbett see his *Letter to Washington* (1796), in *The Complete Writings of Thomas Paine* (hereafter *Writings*), ed. Philip S. Foner (New York: Citadel Press), vol. II, p. 710n.

11. *Porcupine's Works*, vol. IV, pp. 112-13. Cobbett's brief life of Paine was abstracted from a larger work by George Chalmers (pseudonym Francis Oldys), published in 1791.

12. *Porcupine's Works*, vol. IV, pp. 79, 87, vol. V, p. 165; PR, 8 January 1803, p. 2.

13. See the 'Prospectus' to Cobbett's daily newspaper *The Porcupine* (1800-1) (British Library).

14. PR, 19 May 1821, pp. 479-80.

15. Ibid. The *Register* reads 1814 rather than 1804. However internal evidence, such as the reference to 'having so recently witnessed labourers in America' suggests the earlier date. See Dyck, 'William Cobbett', ch. 2.

16. He was imprisoned for 'seditious' criticism of flogging in the military.

17. See Claribel Young, 'A Re-examination of William Cobbett's Opinions of Thomas Paine', *Journal of the Rutgers University Library*, vol. XXXIX, pt. I (1977), pp. 19-21.

18. PR, 19 September 1810, pp. 388-9; PR, 6 July 1811, pp. 3-10; *Paper against Gold* (1810-5), passim.; PR, 10 October 1810, pp. 577-86; PR, 17 October 1810, pp. 643-5, 651.

19. 2 November 1816 is usually said to be the starting date of the cheap *Register*. In fact the first cheap *Register* was dated 12 October 1816.

20. Cobbett, *A History of the Last Hundred Days of English Freedom* (1817), ed. J.L. Hammond (London: Labour Publishing Company, 1921), p. 28. The Home Office Papers for 1817 contain numerous complaints from local

magistrates about the widespread circulation of the two-penny *Register*. Cobbett believed that a circulation of 200,000 had been reached at the end of the first month. See *Hundred Days*, pp. 24, 28; M.L. Pearl, *William Cobbett: A Bibliographical Account of His Life and Times* (1953) (Westport, Conn.: Greenwood, 1971), p. 68; *The Times* 1 January 1818; Spater, *Cobbett*, p. 565n. 108.

21. PR, 2 November 1816, pp. 545-6, 561.

22. PR, 6 December 1817, p. 1097.

23. PR, 26 May 1821, p. 555.

24. *Common Sense*, in *Writings*, vol. I, p. 45.

25. 'The Present Times: or, Eight Shillings a Week' (W. Pratt, printer: Birmingham) (Cambridge University Library: Madden Collection), 21 (VI). The song dates from c. 1825.

26. 'Bonny England, O!' (Phillips and Co., printer: Brighton) (Madden Collection, 22 (VII)).

27. PR, 21 August 1824, pp. 474-5.

28. 'Reminiscences of James Watson' (1854), in *Testaments of Radicalism*, ed. David Vincent (London: Europa, 1977), p. 110.

29. Paine was commonly maligned in songs and 'religious' tracts composed by the ruling class, especially from the 1790s to the 1830s. Examples can be found in the collections of broadsides and ephemeral literature at the British Library, the Bodleian Library and the University of London Library.

30. PR, 27 January 1820, pp. 736-7.

31. PR, 21 December 1822, pp. 707-10.

32. Cobbett to Thomas Hulme, 5 December 1817 (New York Public Library: Emmett Collection). The project was never completed, but he did compose a brief sketch of Paine's life.

33. For an account of the episode see PR, 18 September 1819, pp. 131-2; PR, 13 November 1819, pp. 382-4; Spater, *Cobbett*, pp. 376-9, 384-9, 532. For further accounts of the event see Leo Bessler, 'Peter Porcupine and the Bones of Thomas Paine', in *Pennsylvania Magazine of History and Biography*, vol. 82, no. 2 (1958), pp. 176-85; Claribel Young, 'A Re-Examination of William Cobbett's Opinions of Thomas Paine', *Journal of the Rutgers University Library*, vol. 39, pt. I (1977), pp. 22-3.

34. Spater, *Cobbett*, p. 387; PR, 27 January 1820, pp. 779-83.

35. The bones remained in the house at Cobbett's Normandy Farm until 1844, it would appear. See Alexander Somerville, *The Whistler at the Plough* (London: Charles Gilpin, 1852), p. 305. But also see M.L. Pearl, *Cobbett*, p. 205n.

36. PR, 19 February 1820, pp. 46-52; PR, 8 September 1821, pp. 547-50; PR, 15 September 1821, pp. 593-5.

37. See *Cobbett's Sermons* (1821-2).

38. 'To the Electors of Preston' (1826) (Fitzwilliam).

39. PR, 27 January 1820, p. 746.

40. *The Age of Reason* (1794), in *Writings*, vol. I, p. 464.

41. PR, 27 March 1819, p. 833; PR, 12 July 1817, p. 471. See, too, Cobbett's *History of the Protestant 'Reformation' in England and Ireland* (1824-7).

42. PR, 9 November 1822, p. 332; PR, 3 November 1821, pp. 1066-7.

43. 'My attachment is to all the world, and not to any particular part' (*Crisis* VII, in *Writings,* vol. I, p. 146).

44. 'To the People of England on the Invasion of England' (1804), *Writings,* vol. II, pp. 675-83.

45. 'Important Considerations to the People of This Kingdom' (1803). Cobbett did not confess to the authorship of this tract until 1809.

46. PR, 9 November 1822, p. 325; PR, 2 November 1833, p. 260.

47. PR, 20 August 1831, p. 495.

48. PR, 2 June 1832, p. 545.

49. *The New York Daily Tribune,* 22 July 1853, p. 5.

6 Collaborators of a Sort: Thomas Paine and Richard Carlile

Joel. H. Wiener

No more shall kings, Columbia's sons command,
No more oppression there shall be obey'd,
'Tis England now, that feels her iron hand;
But hope still lives for Paine is not yet dead:
His voice is heard through all this hapless Isle,
He lives, he breathes, he speaks in R. Carlile.

Allen Davenport[1]

Between 1817 and 1826 the radical journalist Richard Carlile published all of the major political and theological writings of Thomas Paine, many of which had not been available since the 1790s. Most were issued in cheap editions; some were circulated widely. In the struggle with the government and private associations over the publication of these tracts, Carlile and several dozen of his shopmen and vendors were imprisoned. In the process, Paine's name again became a byword for radical activism, as it had been to a striking degree in the 1790s when the country was flooded with his tracts, and when plebeian Radicals enthusiastically championed his ideas.[2] Carlile also sought to construct a new radical consensus of artisans and the poor based upon the ideas of Paine. He attempted to lead a crusade against monarchy and priestcraft, two of Paine's *bêtes noires*. In the short term, this movement failed. Yet clearly, Carlile's intimate connection with Paine became a central part of the legacy to reformers in nineteenth-century England.

What precisely was this legacy of Paine as transmitted by Carlile? Did it make a permanent impact on English culture and on working-class reformers in particular? What were its ideological contours? Historians are in considerable disagreement about the answers to these questions. Several of them take the view that the Paine-Carlile influence on reform in the early nineteenth century was substantial, especially in the area of popular freethought. Edward Royle maintains that the 'Paineite infidel tradition' (which he believes lasted until the 1890s, when it was supplanted by socialism) 'might not have existed if Carlile had not revived it after the French wars'.[3] Gwyn A. Williams concludes that it was 'Carlile's massive, heroic, splenetic and idiosyncratic labours in the 1820s which in effect created the "historical" Paine for British readers'.[4] Similarly, though in more general terms, Christopher Hill observes that the reprinting of Paine's writings by Carlile 'played a big part in moulding working-class thought'.[5]

Yet other historians, such as E.P. Thompson and John Belchem, who give more attention to politics than religion, are less persuaded of the importance of Carlile as a transmitter of Paine. Thompson depicts Carlile as one element of a fragmented radicalism, and as somewhat ineffectual even at that. He argues that by the later 1820s, 'the Paine-Carlile tradition had acquired a certain stridency and air of unreality'.[6] Belchem emphasises the leading part played by Henry Hunt in the post-1815 reform movement. Hunt was an inveterate opponent of Carlile, and only marginally was he connected—with Paine.[7] Other historians focus upon the publishing war of the 1820s as a central element of the reinvigorated movement for Radical reform without paying too much heed to its ideological underpinnings and, therefore, to a Paine-Carlile 'tradition'.[8] Clearly, the absence of a consensus points up the need for a more precise analysis.

Carlile's publishing activities on behalf of Paine have been studied by several historians, although these activities have not generally received the attention they deserve as a crucial episode in the history of radical journalism. A brief recapitulation of them is necessary before a fuller examination of

Carlile's relationship to Paine can be undertaken. In 1816, Carlile, recently arrived from Devon where he had been a journeyman tinmaker, began to hawk cheap tracts in the streets of London. He did so at least in part as a protest against authority.[9] His opinions lacked as yet an intellectual focus. After commencing this trade, Carlile began to read political books and pamphlets and to be influenced by the natural rights philosophy being expounded by London's many street orators. He wrote several articles for radical journals that drew upon the political ideas of Paine. It was not until December 1817, however, after a brief incarceration for reprinting three parodies by William Hone, that he read Paine's *Age of Reason*. When he did so, the impact was literally enough to last him a lifetime. This book, he later asserted, 'contains a finer system of ethics, and is more calculated to improve and exalt the human faculties than anything which can be congregated or formed from that Book (i.e., the Bible) which it so ably investigates'.[10] Henceforth, Paine was to be for Carlile a beacon of light through the obstacles of political activism, a sure guide to the complexities of politics and theology.

In March 1817 Carlile met William T. Sherwin; this important journalistic partnership enabled him to give practical expression to his enthusiasm for Paine. Sherwin was a brilliant young journalist who had come to London from Northamptonshire, where he had been dismissed from a minor office because of his Paineite sympathies. He and Carlile began a profitable collaboration in 'sedition'. Sherwin agreed to print and finance the distribution of radical pamphlets. Carlile agreed to publish the pamphlets, which meant that he incurred the legal risks of a prosecution. The two men worked harmoniously together for two years. They jointly produced *Sherwin's Weekly Political Register*, a two-penny paper which was a successor to Sherwin's short-lived *Republican*, and it was the *Weekly Political Register* that first signified the re-emergence of Paine as a key element of popular radicalism. Sherwin wrote numerous political leaders for the paper on Paineite themes, some of them being virtual paraphrases of passages from the *Rights of Man*.[11] Carlile penned similar articles under the pseudonym 'A Plebeian'. He also claimed to be the principal drafter of the *Weekly Political Regis-*

ter's leaders: '[Sherwin] was bold, because I was responsible for all his writings and urged him to be bold'.[12]

In August 1817, the revival of Paine commenced in earnest. Carlile and Sherwin began to reprint all of the political writings systematically. During the 1790s, Paine and several of his publishers and printers had been prosecuted by the Pitt government, and from that time on many of his writings could only be obtained clandestinely. Carlile and Sherwin were determined to reclaim for public use as many of his tracts as they could. They began with the political works, which were less likely to draw a prosecution upon them than theological writings like *The Age of Reason*. Half of each number of the *Weekly Political Register* was given over to all or a part of one of Paine's political tracts. *Common Sense*, which had launched Paine's career as a propagandist in 1776 with its ringing assertion that 'the cause of America is in a great measure the cause of all mankind', was the first work to be reprinted. Supported by Sherwin's statement that 'if a Declaration of Independence was justifiable on the part of America; it surely is justifiable on the part of Britain',[13] it created a stir in radical circles. Each of the other major political tracts followed, including Parts I and II of the *Rights of Man*. The publication of the latter was especially significant because it marked the first reprinting in 20 years of a seminal work in political theory that previously had electrified thousands of poor reformers.

The publication of Paine's political tracts followed the format used for *Common Sense*; that is, they appeared initially in the *Weekly Political Register* and were then sold separately in 2d or 3d numbers, depending upon the quality of the paper used. Carlile stressed that he was emulating the example of Paine in making the writings available to poor readers, so that the latter might have a solid foundation on which to organise their political thoughts. He and Sherwin also published a complete two-volume edition of the *Political Works of Thomas Paine* (1817-18) with a portrait of Paine. They lost money on these volumes, which sold for less than £2 although about 2,000 copies were sold. In 1819 Carlile brought out a more expensive edition of Paine's *Political Writings* on his own. He followed this with another edition in 1820 entitled the *Political and Miscellaneous Works*, which included about 100 additional pages of material sent to him by William Clark, an American bookseller. This edition also contained a brief *Life of Thomas Paine* by Carlile, which was based in part on a more substantial biography written and published by Sherwin the year before.[14] When another radical publisher, William Benbow, took advantage of Carlile's imprisonment in Dorchester Gaol to publish an edition of Paine's political writings in 6d numbers in 1821, Carlile reacted indignantly. He had resurrected Paine as a major figure in radical publishing (partly with the assistance of Sherwin) and was not prepared to brook competition from an interloper. However, he was unable to stop Benbow, whose edition seems to have sold poorly.

In 1822, Carlile issued yet another collection of the political writings of Paine. He also published Paine's *Miscellaneous Letters and Essays on Various Subjects* (1819), which included 30 pieces not previously circulated in England. In 1826, he issued a collection of Paine's *Aphorisms, Opinions and Reflections*, put together in lexicographical form. In all, between 1817 and 1826 Carlile made available thousands of copies of Paine's political writings; this was far fewer than had been in circulation during the heady years 1791 to 1794, but it was still an enormous advance upon the furtive reading of Paine that had characterised the interim decades.[15] Carlile's publishing activities gave a stimulus to the revived movement for radical change. As E.P. Thompson makes clear, they also helped to sustain a 'Jacobin tradition' of popular political radicalism that was nourished by the revolutionary natural rights philosophy of the 1790s and was then extended into the 1830s and beyond.[16]

More controversial than Carlile's publication of Paine's political writings was his reprinting of the theological works, beginning in December 1818. From its initial appearance in 1791-4, *The Age of Reason*, particularly Part II, had been condemned as blasphemous by churchmen and conservatives. It had been the object of several prosecutions, and no edition of either part of this work was sold openly in England after 1797.[17] In 1812, Daniel Eaton, a plebeian journalist, was imprisoned and placed in the pillory for issuing some minor theological writings by Paine, which he described as 'Part Three' of *The Age of Reason*. Since that time no attempt had been made to publish any of the 'blasphemous' writings of Paine. Carlile now sought to reverse this situation, making it the chief focus of his journalistic activities between 1818 and 1820. He was keen to distribute the theological writings because he wanted to throw down the gauntlet of opposition to the Liverpool government over the issue of publishing freedom. What better way to do this than by unleashing the spectre of irreligion, a prospect too dire for even moderate reformers to contemplate. For Carlile the key question was: Are ordinary people who are discontented with their lives to be allowed to scrutinise the foundations of arbitrary government, whether these be secular or religious? If the answer to this question was affirmative, then it might be possible to forge a new radical movement centred on the ideas of Paine. If not, then in Carlile's view England could no longer claim to be a country which permitted the expression of dissenting opinions.

With Sherwin's tacit support, but under his own imprint, Carlile published *The Age of Reason* in December 1818 at a price of 1s 6d. Accompanied by a wave of excitement among reformers, which was increased by a series of prosecutions launched against Carlile, this edition of 1,000 copies sold out within a month. Carlile then brought out a second edition of 3,000 copies to meet the demand, this time without any backing from Sherwin. He also published a bound volume of Paine's *Theological Works* (1818) at 10s 6d, including the controversial 'Part Three' of *The Age of Reason* as well as Parts I and II Prosecutions for blasphemous and seditious libel were directed at Carlile by the Attorney-General and the Society for the Suppression of Vice, but he continued to flaunt his defiance by publishing and selling the banned works.[18] Profits began to roll in, and at a rate unprecedented and never to be repeated for Carlile. Within a year, the legal system caught up with him. After a well-publicised trial in the Guildhall in October 1819, at which he defended *The Age of Reason* and read it verbatim to the jury during the course of a single day, he was convicted of blasphemy. Sentenced to one year in prison and a heavy fine, Carlile spent the next six years in Dorchester Gaol because he refused to accept any legal conditions on his freedom.[19] In so doing, he became the most prominent 'victim' in the entire history of Paine's publications, albeit one who revelled in his situation and became ever more convinced of the rightness of Paine's ideas.

While Carlile was in prison, the Vice Society, the Constitutional Association for Opposing the Progress of Disloyal and Seditious Principles (founded in 1821), and the Tory government continued their renewed war against Paine. They successfully brought charges of blasphemous and seditious libel against Carlile's wife, his sister and many of his shopmen and vendors for publishing and selling Paine's writings. Still, the struggle went on. In 1819-20, from Dorchester Gaol, Carlile issued the *Mock Trials of Richard Carlile*, which included a substantial segment of *The Age of Reason*. He also published the *Deist, or Moral Philosopher*, a two-volume collection of miscellaneous freethought pamphlets which included Elihu Palmer's *Principles of Nature* and several other works strongly influenced by Paine. Carlile followed this up in 1823 with a miniature edition of the *Theological Works* of Paine. He printed 5,000 copies of this edition at a price of 2s 3d, yet made only a small profit. During 1825 and 1826, he published additional collections of Paine's theological writings. No other English publisher circulated any of Paine's theological writings during the 1820s, although there is evidence to indicate that William Benbow published a small edition of some of the more controversial writings for private circulation.

This account of Carlile's energetic publishing activities on behalf of Paine has a decidedly heroic cast to it. Even so, it does not indicate the singleminded intensity which informed it. Carlile identified in an almost personal way with Paine, 'our great and only prototype', and repeatedly paid tribute to him. In his *Life of Thomas Paine*, he compared his own prosecution and imprisonment in 1819 with that initiated against Paine in 1792, which led to the latter's exile from England. Carlile forcefully resisted his prosecutors, at least in part because he believed that he owed it to Paine. He informed the Vice Society in 1819 that 'nor the fear of imprisonment, nor the fear of death shall deter me from a perseverance'.[20] When his wife Jane was convicted for selling Sherwin's *Memoir of the Life of Thomas Paine* in 1820, he wrote: 'The conviction of Mrs. Carlile shall not stop the struggle: the name of Paine shall rise superior to all opposition, and be pronounced the brightest of all the bright ornaments that this country has hitherto produced, and continue so long as Britain shall be visible as an inhabited island.'[21] Paine stood for the principle of free investigation, and he was determined to give effect to this principle as a means of undermining oppression and bigotry. So resolute was Carlile about this that he named his third son 'Thomas Paine'. When the boy died in 1819, he gave the name to his next son. Carlile's house was furnished with a statue of Paine, which was sculpted for him by a radical acquaintance who later turned out to be a police spy. And his Fleet Street shop — the first of several 'Temples of Reason' — was stocked with books and tracts by Paine and by small busts and engravings of his portrait, all of which were for sale. Carlile was a fully matured disciple of Paine by the early 1820s; intellectually and by temperament he was the most dedicated Paineite of the nineteenth century.

Carlile's primary objective was to place Paine at the centre of radical warfare; his hope being that the successes of the 1790s might be repeated. A new generation of workingmen would then be inspired to take up the cry for radical reform. Notwithstanding the republication of Paine's writings, therefore, and the unremitting energy that Carlile gave to this cause, further questions must be asked: To what extent were his political objectives successful? Did he effectively transmit or reinterpret Paine to a new generation of plebeian reformers? Did the accessibility of Paine's writings after 1817 give a renewed impetus to radical reform? Answers to these questions depend upon an analysis of Carlile's ideological borrowings from Paine as well as an assessment of his successes and failures as a practical agitator. They also necessitate that additional consideration be given to the struggle by Carlile and his followers for a free press, since this issue was critical to the revival of Paine.

In his *Republican* (1819-26) and other journals, as well as in the many pamphlets he wrote in the 1820s, Carlile disseminated the ideas of Paine to his artisan and working-class followers. Yet his use of Paine was decidedly selective. He never showed much interest in Paine's economic and social ideas (as important as they were), although he endorsed his attacks upon paper money, the funding system and extravagant public expenditure financed by heavy and unequal taxation. He agreed fully with Cobbett and other radicals who used Paine's economic analyses as the basis for a general attack upon social and political institutions. Paper money, Carlile maintained, was a 'state juggle' that forced up taxation; while heavy government borrowing was 'calculated to swallow up all property in one common vortex, and to make it entirely change hands, by taking from the industrious and supporting the idle and vicious'. The 'fundamental error' was the 'rotten system of credit and paper money', because all financial evils followed from it.[22]

Yet, Carlile eschewed those social reforms advocated by Paine in Part II of the *Rights of Man* and in his influential tract *Agrarian Justice*. These involved pensions for the elderly, child benefits and maternity and funeral allowances.[23] Carlile was not prepared to mount a challenge against any of the institutions that secured private property. His economic world was that of the West Country in the late eighteenth century, where he had grown up, and of a London dominated by artisanal values. His faith was rooted in craftsmen and small producers. He had few ties to the new industrial society. His perspective was individualistic: 'petty bourgeois' to use the terminology of Marxism. It was a world that increasingly was to come under attack from working-class reformers; perhaps in implicit recognition of this, Carlile made little use of Paine in this area.

Much more important to Carlile was his two-pronged assault upon an oppressive political system and a religion based on superstition. In what was a virtual paraphrase of Paine, Carlile maintained that hereditary government and clerical power were interlocked. Both were functions of arbitrary government, and both, he believed, would disintegrate if sufficient pressure was applied to them. He attempted to resuscitate 'Jacobin' political radicalism and to link it to anti-clericalism. Carlile repeatedly urged his followers (who corresponded with him individually and in small groups from every section of the country) to become 'republicans' and 'deists'. In this way, he believed that Paine's ideas could be transmitted effectively to a new generation of radicals to be put to service in the cause of reform.

The political legacy of Paine — as filtered through Carlile's writings in the 1820s — warrants a close analysis. A segment of the 'political Paine' had survived the prosecutions of the

1790s. During the years of the underground 'Jacobin tradition', and in the immediate post-1815 period when England was convulsed by renewed movements for reform, radicals owed at least some of their rhetoric to Paine.[24] The eighteenth-century belief in popular sovereignty, which he had presented in an attractive form, was a central element of radical thought. Furthermore, all radicals paid homage to the ideal of freedom and accepted the need for an extension of the franchise. They also endorsed the principle of an equality of natural rights. In differing ways, this was as true of Major Cartwright and William Cobbett, both of whom looked to the historical past for proper basis of reform, as it was of Henry Hunt, for whom universal suffrage was the touchstone of political change. None of these reformers can be regarded as true disciples of Paine. Yet their adherence to a corpus of 'Paineite' ideas indicates that, independent of Carlile's contribution, Paine's political heritage was in part a general one.[25]

But for Carlile, the true disciple, the ideas of the 'political Paine' were obviously crucial. Paine's writings, he stated forcefully, are 'the only standard political writings that are worth a moment's notice'.[26] He described the *Rights of Man* as a 'monument of political wisdom and integrity',[27] because it set out a rational case for everything that Carlile passionately believed in: universal rights, republicanism, even the summoning of a convention to draft a constitution for England. Carlile told the readers of the *Republican* that monarchy 'should be no longer kept up as an *useless and expensive* establishment'.[28] It had outlived its purpose and must be replaced by popular institutions. Still, he emphasised that the form of government was not critical, as it had not been for Paine. What counted was a spirit of 'republicanism', by which he meant a political structure fashioned in some way by a majority of the people.

During the early 1820s, Carlile became an ardent proponent of republicanism. Arbitrary governments were being toppled in Spain, Portugal and elsewhere, and he foresaw a bright future for Europe. He hoped to avoid revolution at home. But in his view 'revolutions become essential to all countries at stated periods',[29] and if Paine's ideas continued to be ignored by the English ruling class, a harsh political necessity would intervene. Whether peaceably or not, absolute monarchy and its oppressive buttresses, notably the church, had to be removed within a few years.

Between 1819 and 1821, when Carlile appeared to be more concerned with the publication of Paine than with the diffusion of his ideas, his rhetoric was sometimes unrestrained. He relied upon the generalities of Paine, though in crude form, as in his call to the people to take up arms 'for the recovery of their rights, and the defence of their persons'.[30] From 1821 on, his position became better defined. He called on his followers in London and elsewhere to declare themselves 'republicans' and to make the word synonymous with radical reform. The 'elective principle' must be pushed everywhere, he contended, which meant not only that the monarchy and the House of Lords had to be destroyed but that the people must be given the right to select the magistrates. 'The name of Thomas Paine', Carlile wrote, 'is of more value and consequence than that of all the kings on the face of the earth, and all their adherents in the bargain.'[31]

Carlile also wanted his republican supporters to accept Paine's dictum that 'no such thing as a constitution exists, or ever did exist, and consequently ... the people have yet a constitution to form'.[32] At his trial for publishing *The Age of Reason*, he had rested part of his defence upon the claim that blasphemous libel did not exist in the common law because judges defined this law exactly as they wished it to be. 'I do not know what the common law is', Carlile had stated.[33] One way around this obstacle was for the people to demand that a convention be summoned to draft a constitution. Carlile did not consistently endorse this idea. Yet he supported it strongly at times, and many of his supporters took it up, as at Leeds and elsewhere in 1821.[34]

These political ideas — a belief in 'elective' government, and in a convention to give England a proper body of constitutional law and to underscore the principle of universal rights — may not seem very different from those of Hunt and other radicals who stressed the importance of universal suffrage. Yet they led to a major split in the 1820s between the 'Paineites', headed by Carlile, and the supporters of Hunt. This split was exacerbated by personal hostility between Carlile and Hunt, and by their differing views on the subject of religion, for the Carlile-Paine group championed 'infidelity' as well as republicanism. Yet, it also marked a serious political divide between Paineite 'idealism' and the pragmatism of Hunt. Both groups of reformers agreed that priority must be given to political reform (in contrast to the Owenites, who emphasised economic reform). But they were at odds over tactics, with the suffragist enthusiasts being prepared to accept the half a loaf of an extended franchise while Carlile's supporters held out for theological and moral change as well.

In the early 1820s, 'republicans' warred against the supporters of Hunt for control of local political organisations. The Huntites established the Great Northern Radical Union, as an association that sought to elect representatives to Parliament. Carlile's followers, who formed groups like 'The Friends of Universal Liberty of Wakefield' and the 'Birmingham Paine Club', gained the upper hand in a few towns and cities, including Leeds, for a time. Mostly, however, they were beaten badly by the franchise reformers.[35] By 1823, Hunt's Great Northern Radical Union collapsed as subscriptions dried up. At the same time, Carlile's republicans fared worse. They divided into small groups of freethinkers and educational reformers. Some of them defected temporarily from radical politics, to return during the exciting days of Chartism and the unstamped press agitation of the 1830s. Others were a permanent loss to political agitation.

The weaknesses of Carlile's republican movement in the 1820s, which he tried unsuccessfully to revive a decade later, diluted the political legacy of Paine. Reformers could now read Paine's political texts again because Carlile had made them available. But these texts did not provide the centrepiece of a radical campaign, as they had done in the 1790s. To an extent, this was the result of Carlile's ineffectiveness as a political leader. He was incapable of maintaining an agitation for long or of transmitting a cohesive body of ideas to reformers. He quarrelled with other reformers and quickly lost enthusiasm even for his own most favoured projects. Thus he allowed 'republicanism' to peter out, as well as the idea of summoning a convention. In the 1790s large numbers of political reformers, particularly the members of the London Corresponding Society, had been enthusiastic Paineites. This did not happen to the same extent in the 1820s, in part because Paine became too closely identified with Carlile.

Radical reformers continued to champion some of Paine's political ideas in the 1830s — mainly in the unstamped press and in organisations such as the National Union of the Working Classes (1831-5), and in the Chartist movement through the leadership of such men as George Julian Harney.[36] But the political heritage of Paine-Carlile became a weak and fragmented one.

However, the importance of Carlile as a disseminator of Paine's ideas to the working classes rests primarily on 'infidelity', not politics. Carlile never lost his interest in political reform. But from an early stage in his career, he began to see religion as the chief obstacle to reform. Paine's political writings were vital, according to Carlile, but it was by his theological writings that Paine would become 'the real benefactor and the saviour of mankind'.[37] For Carlile, arbitrary rule and oppression were typified above all by the superstitious belief in a God. Theology was linked to politics because both rested on a foundation of privilege. Carlile told his readers that 'we must get rid of all ideas of supernatural powers and places before we can be well fitted to govern ourselves through life as members of society'.[38] Religion was insidious because it obstructed the advancement of knowledge. And knowledge, Carlile believed, was the key to radical reform. Therefore, he attempted to establish a movement of freethinkers (or 'infidels') to undermine the validity and the power of religion. The ideas of Paine were integral to such a movement.

From 1819 to 1821, Carlile acted as a moderate interpreter of Paine's theological views. Although he demurred at Paine's belief in the possibility of an afterlife, and asserted that 'I am the disciple of Paine in politics only',[39] he expounded an ecumenical deism of the kind set out by Paine in Part I of his *Age of Reason*. Paine's deism followed from his belief that 'the vast machinery of the universe' is the result of an act of creation, and that this machinery was 'an ever-existing exhibition of every principle upon which every part of mathematical science is founded'.[40] One such principle was a system of natural ethics: its moral goodness would reveal itself when artificial obstacles to human understanding were eliminated. In paraphrasing Paine, Carlile observed that 'The great First Cause or the Supreme and all influencing Power, which we call God, is omnipotent and all-sufficient, and needs no mediator to intercede with him and his creatures'.[41] Like Paine, he believed that organised religion, particularly Christianity, with its many frauds and superstitutions, stood in the way of achieving this perfectibility. If freethinkers could weaken Christianity, a better world would result. 'Nothing but superstitution', claimed Carlile, 'can now prevent [man] from reaching that summit of happiness, which of all other animals, it is the peculiar blessing of man to enjoy'.[42]

Yet the text of *The Age of Reason*, and the symbolic identification of its author as a veritable Antichrist, carried with them the possibility of a more militant onslaught against religion. In *The Age of Reason*, Paine pointed out the contradictions and inconsistencies of the Jewish and Christian scriptures, and in Part II he expressly rejected the Bible as the word of God. He stated that Christianity was an 'engine of power' which 'serves the purpose of despotism; and ... the avarice of priests; but so far as respects the good of man in general, it leads to nothing here or hereafter'.[43] In chapter after chapter he amassed a significant weight of 'moral evidence' against the Old and New Testaments. A small number of eighteenth-century freethinkers had anticipated such an approach. But Paine gave scriptural criticism an impetus by his outright rejection of revelation and his popular style of expression. As one historian has observed: 'Before Paine it had been possible to be both a Christian and a deist: now such a religious outlook became virtually untenable.'[44]

Within a short period of time, Carlile took up this more militant approach to Christianity. He attempted to give blasphemy and infidelity a cutting edge. Readers of the *Republican* — there were about 5,000 of them by the early 1820s — were regaled with quotations from Paine and *The Age of Reason*, which Carlile described as 'the terror of the Christian world'.[45] During 1820 and 1821, the *Republican* began to read like an extended summary of Paine the scriptural exegete, as Carlile engaged in lengthy 'debates' with defenders of orthodox Christianity. Drawing heavily upon Part II of *The Age of Reason*, he sought to demonstrate the improbabilities of Scripture, including the falsity of 'this tale of the son of the carpenter and a virgin'. He described himself

as an 'Infidel to the Christian religion' and characterised the
Bible as 'one of the most treasonable and seditious books that
ever appeared in print'. 'It is time that the fraud should be
unmasked', he told his readers, 'and it shall be my career
through life to unmask it.'[46] By making effective use of Paine's
technique of the internal analysis of the Scriptures, he spread
freethinking ideas among his readers. That these ideas had an
impact is evident from the extensive correspondence Carlile
undertook with his readers in the pages of the *Republican*.
Many of his readers testified to the influence of *The Age of
Reason* on them personally; others, in growing numbers,
affirmed their belief in Paine's ideas as transmitted by Carlile.
Thus Carlile gave a decided stimulus to popular infidelity,
particularly to that aspect of it which drew its strength from
scriptural criticism.

More passionately, Carlile (purportedly citing Paine) began
to call for the destruction of Christianity. He described priests
as the 'common enemies of mankind' and condemned Christianity in millennialist terms: 'Oh horrible religion, what
havoc hast thou made on the earth! Thou are a pestilence,
more destructive of life, happiness, and peace, than all other
pestilences combined!'[47] His aim was 'to root out this
grievous, useless, ingenious tax (i.e. religion), to destroy this
source of disunion and quarrel, to leave the human mind free
to self-government, and to teach mankind every where to
seek and to value truth'. He urged freethinkers to throw off
their shackles and to 'propagate the principles of Thomas
Paine' as a battering ram against the miseries and inhumani-
ties of 'priestcraft'.[48]

Carlile urged his followers to identify themselves as disciples of Paine. Groups of them, notably artisans in many of
Britain's town and cities and in sections of London, proceeded
to do this. His supporters formed 'Paine Clubs', or organised
themselves as 'Friends of Rational Liberty' or something
similar. They subscribed to his prison expenses, circulated the
writings of the 'immortal Paine' whenever this was possible,
and expressed their loyalty to the cause of infidelity in other
ways. In letters that appeared regularly in the *Republican*,
subscribers vowed to do what they could to 'keep alive the
memory of the hero of liberty' and the 'Apostle of Reason'.[49]
At Carlile's urging, some readers began to celebrate Paine's

birthday on 29 January with toasts, anti-Christian speeches, and songs like 'The Mighty Tom Paine' (sung to the melody of 'Auld Lang Syne') or 'In Liberty's Cause I Could Yield Up My Life'.[50] These infidel events were reported in the *Republican* and discussed by the paper's readers. Some groups of deists and infidels managed to preserve their cultural identity over a considerable period of time, even when confronted by pressures from political and economic associations. Others began to lose their momentum, as is clear from a steady decrease in the reporting of infidel activities in the *Republican* (together with a decline in that paper's circulation), and from an acknowledgement by Carlile and many of his supporters that defections were taking place. None the less, the overall effect for a time was to give an impetus to Paineite thought.

Beginning in 1821, some of Carlile's followers formed zetetic societies. The Greek word 'zetetic' means 'to seek for', and these reformers sought to keep alive the ideas of Paine, though in an educational rather than a political sense. The zetetic societies formally linked Carlile's fortunes to those of Paine. They established reading rooms where the writings of both freethinkers were made available, toasted them jointly on infidel occasions (Carlile's birthday on 8 December became a cause for annual celebration along with Paine's), and did whatever they could to disseminate freethinking ideas. The most active zetetic society was in Edinburgh, where the tradesmen Robert and James Affleck attempted to keep the infidel cause alive against local opposition. Other zetetic societies were founded and maintained in Glasgow, Salford, London, Stallybridge and elsewhere. All of them were held together by the writings of Paine and the journalism of Carlile. A few zetetic societies were reincarnations of deist organisations that had continued to function during the years of underground activity between the 1790s and the 1820s. Most, however, had no links to the past or to other radical organisations. Inspired by the example of Carlile, they aimed to make Paine an integral part of the radical tradition and to keep his ideas in circulation.[51]

The Paine-Carlile legacy is unquestionably more vital in the area of popular freethought than of republicanism. But it is misleading to overemphasise the 'infidel' component of radicalism, particularly in its earlier phase. There are at least two reasons for caution. The first is that within a few years Carlile himself abandoned many of Paine's theological ideas. From militant deism he moved, by the end of 1822, to atheism and materialism, and he began to draw heavily upon the writings of Baron d'Holbach, whose eighteenth-century book *System of Nature* was widely read in the 1820s. By 1822, the *Republican* began to cite d'Holbach's writings extensively, much as it had done with Paine. Thus although *The Age of Reason* continued to represent the plebeian commitment to freethought, it was forced to share centre stage among popular infidels with the writings of d'Holbach and other freethinkers. British secularism, as it developed subsequently under the leadership of George Jacob Holyoake and Charles Bradlaugh, represented a fusion of Paine and materialism. The former continued to hold first place in the pantheon of infidel thought. But by no means was the gap as wide as it had once been.

The other factor to be considered in assessing the freethought legacy of Paine-Carlile is the failure of most of the deist and zetetic associations to survive beyond the 1820s. In part this was due to their inability to resist continuing acts of persecution. In Edinburgh, for example, the zetetic society was charged by the authorities with spreading blasphemy, and its library was confiscated. The Affleck brothers were prosecuted for their anti-Christian activities and imprisoned in 1823. More important was Carlile's conversion to materialism and, from 1827 on, to a form of allegorical deism being expounded by a lapsed Anglican clergyman named Robert Taylor. This produced divisions among his followers and further fragmented popular infidelity. In the early 1830s, Carlile quarrelled with Taylor and then moved on to an esoteric version of freethought which incorporated elements of both Christianity and rationalism.

Once again, Carlile's inconsistent qualities as a leader were a significant factor in weakening Paine's influence. Certainly, Carlile provided a major stimulus to a revitalised Paineite freethought movement in the early 1820s. Yet in practical terms he failed to follow through. He was temperamentally incapable of sustaining a unified reform effort, despite being quite good at providing an initial spark. As Carlile's interest in deism waned, many former Paineites turned to universal suffrage and became enthusiastic supporters of Hunt; others adopted Owenite doctrines or became active in trade unionism or the movement for factory reform; still other infidels (smaller in numbers) attempted to keep the flame alive by means of discussion groups and educational activities. A few of these groups maintained a loose continuity until later in the century, by which time popular freethought had been transformed into a less militant kind of secularism. But most disappeared permanently. Paine's legacy to freethinkers continued to be important. From the 1820s on, *The Age of Reason* remained the single most widely-read anti-Christian text.[52] There are numerous references to it in secularist journals like Holyoake's *Reasoner* and Bradlaugh's *National Reformer*. Yet, a major revival of Paineite irreligion — of the kind that took place in the political sphere in the 1790s — did not occur. Carlile had commenced a struggle only to leave the outcome unfinished.

It has been argued that Paine's legacy to reformers as transmitted by Carlile was not as significant as it might have been, even in the area of infidelity. Yet the belief persists, with considerable evidence to support it, that the legacy was a substantial one. Is the contradiction resolvable? Was the reality less meaningful than some historians have asserted it to be? The seeming contradiction has to do with the emphasis given to Paine's ideas and to Carlile's attempts to give effect to them. Neither the quality of these ideas nor the somewhat fickle commitments of Carlile will bear the weight of this kind of analysis. In the 1820s 'republicanism' was incapable of engendering much enthusiasm among plebeian radicals at a time when the suffrage was extremely limited and when the economic conditions of the poor seemed to be worsening. Similarly, deism, whether of a moderate or militant kind, had only a limited appeal when forced to compete with other kinds of radicalism. It was a product of eighteenth-century thought and, in the view of many radical reformers, did not address itself to concrete issues of power and decision-making. To make infidelity a practical force among English artisans and workingmen a leavening of materialism or Owenite economic analysis was needed. This happened from the mid-1820s on, though even then secularism never became as central to the radical tradition as either political or economic reform.

Yet Paine's heritage, as passed on by Carlile, was significant, and the explanation for this has as much to do with technique and symbolism as content. By means of Paine, Carlile largely won the battle for a free press between 1819 and 1824. Paine's writings were the banner that he and his enthusiastic disciples held aloft as they fought against the attempt to suppress radical ideas.[53] A comparable situation had appeared to be in the making in the 1790s. Paine's objective then had been to further the process of investigation. 'It is error only, and not truth, that shrinks from enquiry', he had declared.[54] Yet the struggle for a free press was soon overshadowed by the revolutionary crisis of the decade, and it ended in an overwhelming defeat for the reformers. In 1792 Paine left England permanently after the prosecution of Part II of the *Rights of Man*. He never returned to contest the sentence of banishment that was proclaimed in his absence. A small number of reformers continued to make eloquent speeches on behalf of a free press, while a handful of booksellers and printers like Thomas Williams and Daniel Eaton published Paine's works in defiance of the Tory government and were punished accordingly.[55]

But the 1790s experienced nothing comparable to the war Carlile and his shopmen and vendors waged for a free press. It was primarily for the right to publish Paine that they endured lengthy prison terms in the 1820s. In the history of radicalism, the first years of the decade were dominated by the battle for a free press. Meetings were convened by reformers, who described the prosecutions of Carlile and his followers as an 'inquisition', a 'most frightful despotism' and so on. James Watson, who began his career as one of Carlile's shopmen and later became a publisher of Paine's works and a leading secularist, made clear the connection between Carlile and Paine in this struggle. He told a group of Leeds deists in 1821: 'Though young in years, I hope to have the principles of the immortal Paine and Carlile so engraven on my heart, that the iron hand of corruption will never be able to erase them.'[56] Another Leeds shopman, Humphrey Boyle, saluted Paine as a 'Citizen of the World'. '[Paine's] memory is now cherished by all who are great and good', asserted Boyle, 'and may the day not be far distant, when every individual on the face of the earth, will be made fully sensible of the inestimable principles he developed'.[57]

After a series of legal actions between 1819 and 1822, which involved his imprisonment and the confiscation of his stocks of Paine's writings, Carlile believed that the prosecutions were coming to an end. Then, in May 1824, a renewed struggle began. Both the Attorney-General and the Solicitor to the Treasury brought charges of blasphemous libel against several of Carlile's shopmen because of their continuing attempts to distribute the works of Paine and Elihu Palmer. A series of trials took place, which were widely publicised in the *Republican*. Reformers became aroused over the issue of a free press. Francis Place , a notably discreet freethinker, characterised the prosecutions of the 'Newgate martyrs' as 'unjust as they are infamous'.[58] The editor of the *Newgate Monthly Magazine*, who was imprisoned for selling *The Age of Reason*, described them as the 'last grand struggle of dying priestcraft ... [and] the last effort to chain the freedom of the press'.[59] All of the shopmen brought to trial for selling the works of Paine were convicted and sent to prison. Yet this proved to be the last occasion in England's history when press freedom was an issue of such importance to radical reformers. Prosecutions for blasphemous libel declined significantly after 1824 and Paine's writings were never again the object of a prosecution in England.

The outcome of this struggle was, obviously, more of a testament to Carlile than Paine. The latter was a brilliant populariser of ideas, though hardly a courageous symbol of resistance to harsh laws. His fixity of purpose was brought into question on more than one occasion, as when he fled to France in 1792 rather than contest the government's prosecution of *The Age of Reason*. Carlile was the obverse of this. His ideas were shallow and susceptible to sudden shifts. They were less in tune with the prevailing chords of radicalism as the years passed. Nor was Carlile an effective political leader, although he was a good journalist. Still, he was willing to commit everything to a cause. In the 1820s, the most important cause for him was not republicanism or infidelity. It was the free investigation of ideas — the right to publish whatever he chose within reason, however critical it was of those in power. Paine's controversial writings allowed Carlile to proffer this claim in earnest. As collaborators of a sort in the crucial battle for a free press, the two men will remain indissolubly linked.

Notes

1. *Republican*, 24 January 1823. It is reprinted in Edward Royle (ed.), *The Infidel Tradition: From Paine to Bradlaugh* (London: Macmillan, 1976), pp. 36-7.

2. On the impact of Paine's publications in the 1790s, see Albert Goodwin, *The Friends of Liberty: The English Democratic Movement in the Age of the French Revolution* (London: Hutchinson, 1979), pp. 173-9; Gwyn A. Williams, *Artisans and Sans-Culottes: Popular Movements in France and Britain during the French Revolution* (London: Edward Arnold, 1968), pp. 13-18, 58-80. Philip Anthony Brown observes that 'the pamphlets of Paine and his imitators agitated minds wherever reading and booksellers had spread' (*The French Revolution in English History* (London: Crosby, Lockwood and Son, 1918), p. 64). For a negative view of the Paine 'mania', see W.H. Reid, *The Rise and Dissolution of the Infidel Societies in this Metropolis* (London: J. Hatchard, 1800) pp. 1-58.

3. Edward Royle, *Victorian Infidels: The Origins of the British Secularist Movement, 1791-1866* (Manchester: Manchester University Press, 1974), p. 34; Royle, *Infidel Tradition*, p. 70.

4. Introduction to Royle, *Infidel Tradition*, p. xi.

5. 'The Norman Yoke' in *Democracy and the Labour Movement*, ed. John Saville (London: Lawrence and Wishart, 1954), p. 53.

6. E.P. Thompson, *The Making of the English Working Class* (London: Victor Gollancz, 1963), p. 763.

7. Belchem describes Carlile as the propagandist for a 'purist and individualist radicalism' and as the 'prophet of a counter-hegemonic ideology of infidel-republicanism' (John Belchem, *'Orator' Hunt: Henry Hunt and English Working-Class Radicalism* (Oxford: Clarendon Press, 1985), p. 7).

8. See Joel H. Wiener, *Radicalism and Freethought in Nineteenth-Century Britain: The Life of Richard Carlile* (Westport, Ct.: Greenwood Press, 1983), and two earlier works: William H. Wickwar, *The Struggle for the Freedom of the Press in England, 1819-1832* (London: George Allen and Unwin, 1928), and G.D.H. Cole, *Richard Carlile, 1790-1843* (London: Victor Gollancz, 1943).

9. An ironic aspect of Carlile's early life in the West Country is the adolescent pastime he and his companions engaged in: burning effigies of Thomas Paine.

10. *The Report of the Proceedings of the Court of King's Bench ... Being the Mock Trials of Richard Carlile, for Alleged Blasphemous Libels* (London: Richard Carlile, 1822), p. 79.

11. Here is an example of such a leader: 'The People are the origin of all just power; that all power, whatever it may call itself, which does not

emanate from the People, is unjust, and contrary to the RIGHTS OF MAN; and that consequently the People of every Nation have a right to make what alteration or amendment they think proper, either in their form of Government, or in anything else, with which their welfare is concerned, or connected' (*Sherwin's Weekly Political Register*, 5 October 1817).

12. *To the Reformers of Great Britain*, 13 October 1821.

13. *Sherwin's Weekly Political Register*, 23 August 1817.

14. Sherwin's *Memoir of the Life of Thomas Paine* (London: Richard Carlile, 1819) was a major work of rehabilitation for Paine. Sherwin wrote: 'In political enquiry [Paine] was without an equal, and in theological discussion he has laboured more efficiently than any other man to free the world from the trammels of intolerance, prejudice and superstition' (p. 228).

15. The various editions are difficult to locate. But there are fine collections at the British Museum, in the Cole Collection at Nuffield College, Oxford, and in the Thomas Paine Collection at the Thetford Public Library.

16. William Perry of Stockport spoke for many workingmen when he wrote to Carlile that 'I recollect when I purchased the Political Works of Mr. Paine, my means was very scanty, but so determined was I to put them in the hands of my children, that I deprived myself of both butter, sugar, and tea. I purchased them as Mr. Sherwin published them, I do not find my body is any the worse for it, but I find a great pleasure in possessing them, and think myself happy that I have it in my power to teach my children the true path of Republicanism . . .' (*Republican*, 5 April 1822).

17. The strength of feeling against *The Age of Reason* was reflected by a writer who claimed that it posed the question of 'whether the bulwark of our country, the Christian religion, was still to retain its lofty pre-eminence; or whether the floodgates of infidelity were to be unbarred, and these once happy realms left as a beacon to surrounding nations, a prey to desolation' (*Constitutional Remarks Addressed to the People of Great Britain* (London: J. Hatchard & Son, 1819), pp. 52-3).

18. The Vice Society's Bill of Indictment described *The Age of Reason* as a book of 'lies, wickedness, and blasphemy', and characterised Carlile as 'an evil disposed and wicked person' for publishing Paine (*Vice Versus Reason: A Copy of the Bill of Indictment Against Richard Carlile, for Publishing Paine's 'Age of Reason'* (1819)). Carlile's temperate response was as follows: 'Have you no priests in your society? Why do you not set them to write a volume of the same size to refute the arguments and assertions of Paine? I will pledge myself to sell it with the other' (Richard Carlile, *A Letter to the Society for the Suppression of Vice* (London: Richard Carlile, 1819), p. 6).

19. The trial stirred considerable enthusiasm for the cause of freedom of publishing and, indirectly, for the writings of Paine. For a full account, see Wiener, *Radicalism and Freethought*, pp. 33-50. An interesting sidelight to the trial was the confession by the venerable reformer, Major Cartwright, that he read *The Age of Reason* for the first time after hearing of the prosecution of Carlile. (John Cartwright to Thomas Northmore, ca. February 1819, in F.D. Cartwright, *The Life and Correspondence of Major John Cartwright* (London, 1826), vol. II, p. 156.)

20. *Letter to the Society for the Suppression of Vice*, p. 3.

21. *Republican*, 27 October 1820.

22. *Republican*, 9 June 1820; *Lion*, 12 December 1828. Paine's criticism of paper money is to be found in Part I of the *Rights of Man*, in the *Prospects on the Rubicon* (1787), and especially in the *Decline and Fall of the English System of Finance*.

23. H.T. Dickinson describes Paine's social programme as 'the most original contribution to the whole reform movement' (*Liberty and Property: Political Ideology in Eighteenth-century Britain* (London: Weidenfeld and Nicolson, 1977), p. 266). The followers of Thomas Spence adopted some of Paine's radical agrarian ideas in the years after 1815.

24. E.P. Thompson maintains that groups of Paineites continued to meet between the 1790s and post-1815. But his evidence is sketchy and he seems at times to equate Paine with the entire French revolutionary tradition. See *Making of the English Working Class*, pp. 497-9.

25. John Derry effectively brings out the general influence of Paine's ideas: 'Paine bequeathed a substantial legacy to the Radical tradition: a distrust of habitual attitudes and conventional practices; a scepticism towards establishment institutions; a distaste for monarchy; an admiration for America; a belief that society functioned according to discernible principles, whose operation ancient traditions and received superstitions thwarted; a dislike of taxation; a suspicion of government intervention; a faith in the goodness of men and a conviction that the folly of governments is the cause of unhappiness; a hatred of religious establishments; a preference for free trade, and a confidence that trade brought nations together in peaceful understanding' (Derry, *The Radical Tradition: Tom Paine to Lloyd George* (London: Macmillan), 1967), p. 44).

26. *Prompter*, 27 November 1830.

27. Richard Carlile, *Life of Thomas Paine*, 2nd edn (London: Richard Carlile, 1821), p. xvii.

28. *Republican*, 26 May 1820.

29. *Republican*, 3 December 1819.

30. *Republican*, 10 September 1819.

31. *Republican*, 4 January 1822.

32. *Rights of Man*, Part I, in *The Writings of Thomas Paine*, ed. Moncure Daniel Conway (New York: G.P. Putnam's Sons, 1894-6), vol. IV, p. 310. Henceforth this edition of Paine is referred to as the 'Conway edition'.

33. *Report of the Proceedings ... Being the Mock Trials of Richard Carlile*, p. 30.

34. For the position of his Leeds supporters, see Richard Carlile, *An Effort to Set at Rest Some Little Disputes and Misunderstandings between the Reformers of Leeds* (London: Richard Carlile, 1821). Carlile claimed that a convention would become a 'great national school, whence every inhabitant of the country would deserve useful instruction, merely by watching the actions of those who represent it' (*Republican*, 1 December 1820). The best general treatment of the question of a convention is in T.M. Parsinnen, 'Association, Convention and Anti-Parliament in British Radical Politics, 1771-1848', *English Historical Review*, vol. 88 (1973), pp. 504-33.

35. The most detailed coverage of this local political warfare is in Belchem, *'Orator' Hunt*, pp. 143-57.

36. On the 1830s, see Patricia Hollis, *The Pauper Press: A Study in Working-Class Radicalism of the 1830s* (London: Oxford University Press, 1970), pp. 203-19, and Joel H. Wiener, *The War of the Unstamped: The Movement to Repeal the British Newspaper Tax, 1830-1836* (Ithaca, New York: Cornell University Press, 1969), pp. 211-14. The link between the 'political Paine' and Chartism has not been studied systematically. But most histories of Chartism include references to Paine and to his influence on individual Chartists.

37. *Republican*, 17 September 1819.

38. *Republican*, 1 February 1822. He also wrote: 'Witchcraft, priestcraft, kingcraft, and devilcraft, must all fall together ... They have been one and all built on the ignorance, fear, and credulity of mankind, and cannot withstand the progress of education' (*Republican*, 11 August 1820).

39. *Republican*, 16 June 1820. Carlile scoffed at Paine's 'sensual and childish idea of a paradisaical future state' (*Republican*, 8 September 1820). Paine's position on an afterlife was set out in 'My Private Thoughts on a Future State', which was usually sold as 'Part Three' of *The Age of Reason*.

40. *The Age of Reason* in *Writings* (Conway Edition), vol IV, pp. 31-53.

41. *Republican*, 3 December 1819.

42. *Republican*, 7 April 1820.

43. *Writings* (Conway edition), vol. IV, p. 190.

44. Eric Foner, *Tom Paine and Revolutionary America* (New York: Oxford University Press, 1976), p. 247.

45. *Republican*, 14 January 1820.

46. *Republican*, 4 February 1820, 1 October 1819, 8 September 1820.

47. *Republican*, 16 June 1820.

48. *Republican*, 12 August 1824; *To the Reformers of Great Britain*, 20 December 1821.

49. *Republican*, 13 October 1821, 15 February 1822.

50. One song composed by John Smithson of Leeds had the following lyrics:

> For brave Carlile has fairly proved
> > Beyond all doubt or fear.
> That more you persecute the *truth*
> > The brighter 'twill appear;
> And more your minions persevere
> > Their wretched ends to gain,
> The more the people will revere
> > CARLILE AND THOMAS PAINE.

> > > > *Republican*, 11 January 1822

On infidel culture generally, see Royle, *Victorian Infidels*, pp. 203-33, and the interesting essay by Eileen Yeo, 'Robert Owen and Radical Culture' in *Robert Owen: Prophet of the Poor*, eds Sidney Pollard and John Salt (London: Macmillan, 1971), pp. 84-114.

51. Information about the zetetic societies is to be found primarily in the pages of the *Republican*. In his introduction to Royle, *Infidel Tradition*, Gwyn A. Williams characterises the zetetics as 'the nursery for a whole generation

of working-class infidels' (p. xi). Elsewhere Edward Royle and James Walvin describe them as the 'heirs to the Paineite Jacobin tradition' (*English Radicals and Reformers, 1760-1848* (Brighton: Harvester Press, 1982), p. 131).

52. Susan Budd, *Varieties of Unbelief: Atheists and Agnostics in English Society, 1850-1960* (London: Heinemann, 1977), pp. 107-11. On the continuity of infidel activity, see Royle, *Victorian Infidels*, especially pp. 149-249, and Edward Royle, *Radicals, Secularists, and Republicans: Popular Freethought in Britain, 1866-1915* (Manchester: Manchester University Press, 1980), especially pp. 45-71, 88-148.

53. Wickwar, *Struggle for the Freedom of the Press*, observes perceptively that 'it was the Press rather than the works of Paine that formed the central object of [Carlile's] devotion' (p. 5).

54. *Letter Addressed to the Addressers on the Late Proclamation*, in *Writings* (Conway edition), vol. IV, p. 59.

55. On the press prosecutions of the 1790s,, see particularly Goodwin, *Friends of Liberty*, pp. 271-4.

56. *Republican*, 11 January 1822.

57. *Republican*, 20 September 1822.

58. Place, *St Paul the Apostle, and William Campion* (1824), in *Republican*, 25 June 1824.

59. *Newgate Monthly Magazine*, 1 August 1826.

7 The Legacy of Thomas Paine

George Spater

At the time of Paine's death in 1809 his great works, *Common Sense*, *Rights of Man* and *The Age of Reason*, had almost disappeared from sight. A prospective purchaser of any of these writings would have been hard pressed to find copies in America or England, unless perhaps in a second-hand bookstall. With a single exception, the last edition of these once-popular works had been in 1797, a dozen years before Paine's death.[1] There were, no doubt, copies on shelves in many a home — copies that were still being read and discussed — but all outward signs of a public demand for these writings of Paine had ceased.[2]

In America the political issue of the day was no longer the one to which Paine had devoted so much of his attention: the desirability of a republican government. The current question was whether such a government could effectively be administered. John Adams wrote that 'Our new government is an attempt to divide a sovereignty ... It cannot, therefore, be expected to be very stable or very firm.'[3] And on the religious front, the spirited revival at the close of the eighteenth century had driven infidelity underground.[4] Therefore, 'Paine lingered on in ignominy which would have made his championship injurious to even a popular cause.'[5]

The apparent disinterest in Paine in England was due to quite different reasons. The country was still at war with France — that extraordinary war that dragged along for 22 years, ending only with the battle of Waterloo in 1815. The repressive measures of the government, beginning with the prosecution of Paine in 1792, had been expanded to include the imprisonment of vendors and publishers, the hounding to near-extinction of the reform societies and the suspension of the Habeas Corpus act from 1794 to 1801. These measures, together with the vigorous counter-revolutionary movement among the Methodists after 1795,[6] effectively smothered signs of radical dissent in politics and religion.

Since Paine's assault on the administration in 1791 the Pitt government had assiduously built up a supporting press which assisted to sap the strength of opposition propaganda. The ministers had managed to win over one strong Whig paper by annual subsidies, and in 1792 it founded two more government newspapers, the *True Briton* and the *Sun*.[7] The government offensive was aggressively spearheaded by the *Anti-Jacobin*, or *Weekly Examiner*, founded by George Canning and several other Pitt admirers in 1797, and by the *Anti-Jacobin Review and Magazine*, founded in the following year as a further challenge to the government's critics. Thus by the close of the century the outlet for the expression of liberal opinion in England had been whittled down to a fraction of what had prevailed in 1791.

The political scene had been suddenly and dramatically altered. In 1791 French principles had been at the centre of debate, and they had been sympathetically viewed by a healthy Whig party led by Charles James Fox. But the Whigs were splintered in 1794 when the Duke of Portland and his friends joined the Pitt administration, leaving Fox with a battered following that could rarely muster 70 votes in the House of Commons. From a newsworthy point of view, Paine had become a figure of the past. The *Anti-Jacobin* in 1801 poured its venom upon Dissenters and Roman Catholics — all were capable of treason: 'the name of a disaffected person, and that of a Dissenter are generally synonymous', it declared.[8] Paine was occasionally scored as a deist and a drunkard, but his allegations against the monarchy and aristocracy — the allegations for which he had been outlawed — were seldom if ever mentioned.[9] The anti-Paine propaganda made his name anathema in polite society.

The revival of Paine's controversial writings in England

began several years after his death and continued throughout the decade 1810-20. This was the Regency period, commonly thought of as an age of elegant living as exemplified by the Prince Regent whose wine bill alone came to £8,000 a year. Yet there have been few decades in English history in which the country was so torn by discontent. The long wars had brought unparalleled inflation and a drastic dislocation of men and industry. The peace in 1815 brought an alarming deflation and an even more drastic dislocation of workers and employers. But nature had a hand too. In this period, and continuing until the middle of the century, the rapidly growing population faced periodic food shortages as the result of the wild vagaries of the weather.

In 1810 a large number of banks failed. In 1811 and 1812 widespread unemployment developed among textile workers in the industrial Midlands. At the close of the war, thousands of agricultural workers were without work, and the mounting horde of hungry and idle were augmented by the demobilisation of the armed forces. The unemployed refused to suffer peaceably. Textile machinery was destroyed and obdurate employers were besieged by the Luddite uprisings of 1811 and 1812. More than 20 convicted Luddites were hanged in 1813. 'Bread or Blood' riots broke out in towns and villages in 1816. 'It was', reported William Cobbett, 'a state of confusion approximating a civil war.'[10] It resembled a war indeed; the government's response to the riots was to meet force with greater force.

Cobbett and his principal radical associates, John Cartwright and Henry Hunt, mounted a vigorous campaign to funnel the distress into peaceful channels. The main argument of the Radicals was that the House of Commons should be made more representative of the people through the adoption of universal suffrage. Petitions calling for such reform were being prepared for the new Parliament which was to convene in January 1817. Somewhere between 600,000 and a million signatures (the larger figure representing almost a quarter of the adult male population of England) were obtained. But in the month before Parliament was to meet, a large gathering in support of universal suffrage, held in the heart of London at Spa Fields, erupted into a riot of sufficient proportion to provide the ministry with an excuse to crack down. And crack down it did. The petitions were forgotten. The Habeas Corpus act was once more suspended in 1817, and Cobbett quietly left for America. The repressive policy reached its peak two years later when a large crowd, peacefully gathered at St Peter's Field in Manchester to petition for parliamentary reform, was assaulted by a detachment of mounted yeomanry, which killed eleven and wounded 400 or 500 of the crowd. As if to justify the unjustifiable savagery of the Peterloo Massacre, the government quickly pressed six new measures through Parliament, including a bill which outlawed all meetings of more than 50 persons unless approved by the authorities.

The turmoil within England was paralleled by political disruption outside the country. Beginning in 1810, one after another of Spain's colonies in South America declared their freedom. Spain itself experienced an internal rebellion in 1820. In 1821 the Greeks revolted against the Turks. Surely these events were somwhow related: Cobbett for one saw a 'great moral cause at work'.[11] It seemed as if the French Revolution had begun to work its magic again.

It was out of this welter of revolutionary emotion that Paine was reborn. In 1810 the *Rights of Man* was for the first time translated into Spanish, and in the following year extracts were circulated in Venezuela where the South American revolutions had started.[12] In 1811, a London printer, Daniel Isaac Eaton, published the so-called third part of Paine's *Age of Reason*. Cobbett claimed that Eaton's prosecution caused him (and how many others?) to read the original parts of *The Age of Reason* — a copy of which he had owned since about 1796 but claimed never to have read.[13] With increasing frequency, laudatory references to Paine and his work began appearing in the weekly issues of Cobbett's *Political Register*.[14] In 1817, amidst the rising fever of the reform campaign, the collected political works of Paine in two volumes were published by William Sherwin, and in the following year, Sherwin's associate, Richard Carlile, published Paine's theological works, including the original *Age of Reason*. Other editions were printed in 1819, 1822, 1826 and 1827. Prosecutions followed as a matter of course, giving valuable free advertising to the writings, and focusing the attention of a new generation on their almost forgotten author. Carlile, who was a major force in creating what Gwyn Williams has called the 'historical' Paine,[15] not only fearlessly published Paine's works, but tirelessly lectured on the subject of Paine's freethought, with the unfortunate result that he spent a large part of his adult life in prison.

Two biographies of Paine had been written up to this time, both unfriendly: the Chalmers life in 1791 and the Cheetham life in 1809. Now, in response to the renewed interest in Paine, the Cheetham life was reprinted in London in 1817, and again, in abbreviated form, in 1820, while John Harford produced a life in 1819 (reprinted twice in 1820) specifically designed to show the relationship between Paine's writings and 'the avowed objects of . . . the radicals of 1819'. Paine's admirers struggled to meet this challenge, producing three new biographies in as many years which presented Paine in a more favourable light. These biographies — by Sherwin (1818), Thomas 'Clio' Rickman (1819) and Carlile (1820) — meant that a purchaser now had five biographies of Paine to choose from.

Nor was this the last time the Tom Paine movement was to re-emerge. The post-war troubles of the early 1820s were succeeded by a brief commercial boom that peaked in 1825; 1829 brought a 'sudden relapse into deep depression', and the 1830s were characterised by a new wave of discontent. In 1830-1, the agricultural workers burned and pillaged under the endorsement of the mythical 'Captain Swing', while reform agitation rocked the major cities of the Midlands; and in 1837-8, thousands marched in support of the Chartist movement seeking universal suffrage, a secret ballot and more equitable parliamentary representation. Outside England there had been recent rebellions in Belgium, Poland and France. The pattern of a dozen years earlier was repeated. Paine's *Rights of Man* was reprinted in England and Scotland in 1830, 1832, 1833 and 1837. The Charter was published with a copy of the *Rights of Man* attached. New editions of *Common Sense* appeared.

After the reform agitations of the 1830s, the influence of Paine on specific reform objectives becomes more difficult to trace. The prosecution of publishers and booksellers stopped, and the publication of Paine's works, which continued throughout the balance of the nineteenth century, and up to the present in the current century, proceeded in leisurely fashion rather than in sudden spurts responsive to political emergencies.

Devoted expositors of Paine's views were found in George Jacob Holyoake (1817-1906) and Charles Bradlaugh (1833-91), who, like their inspirational leader, combined the propaganda of freethought in religion with republican radicalism in politics, and left their mark in the numerous secular societies that flourished throughout Great Britain from the 1850s.[16] The societies were influential in seeing that Paine's birthday, 29 January, was appropriately celebrated each year. In 1890 one of the secular society branches 'held a children's Thomas Paine birthday tea party, with food, music and a magic-lantern show; and at the close each child was given a printed memorial card on which was fixed a photograph of the immortal Paine'.[17] Paine was the original hero — the Adam, the Moses, the Jove — in the pantheon of the English worker. The banners of striking miners in county Durham in 1875 displayed the portraits of those responsible for the making of the working class: Thomas Paine (the initiator of the agitation of the 1790s), Henry Hunt (the speaker at the scene of the Peterloo Massacre of 1819) and Ernest Jones and Feargus O'Connor (the leaders of the Chartist movement of the 1830s and 40s).[18] A Paine Memorial Hall was erected in London. The Thomas Paine Society was formed in 1963, and in the following year a statue of Paine was raised at Thetford, his birthplace.

Although the image of Thomas Paine as a radical reformer was carried along from one generation to the next over a very long period — from corresponding societies in the 1790s to zetetics, Owenites, Chartists and secularists — Paine's ideas were never institutionalised, so each generation took what it wanted from the teachings of the master. By the 1890s, the working-class movement had gone off in an entirely different direction from that visualised by Paine. He had levelled his attacks on 'kingcraft' and 'priestcraft'; but as industrialism expanded, the working man came to see the capitalist employer as a more immediate evil. The trade union became the prevailing mode of association and socialism became the prevailing ideology. 'Paine was no longer the founding father — he had been displaced by Marx.'[19] His *Age of Reason*, however, continued into the twentieth century as a primer of freethought propaganda.[20]

Paine's continuing political influence can be assessed only on a broad scale. The society that he addressed was a society that generally accepted the *status quo*. The good things in the world were for the elite. The labouring classes took for granted an inferior position for themselves and their progeny. Paine, more than any one else, showed that this did not have to be. His objective was true equality — an objective to be secured by revolution — and this was a widely accepted solution among the working class. When Robert Louis Stevenson crossed the Atlantic in 1879 he found that to the steerage passengers 'the cause of everything in England was the form of government, and the cure for all evils was, by consequence, a revolution'.[21]

While there has been no abrupt revolutionary explosion in England, the tables have slowly turned, and are still slowly turning, towards a greater degree of equality since Paine made his stand 200 years ago. The gradual shift of influence away from the minority, which had held an unassailable dominance for centuries, is without doubt the greatest political change in recorded history. Paine must forever take first rank among those who precipitated the shift.

Thus the working-class movement in England owes a far greater debt to Paine than can be found in any identifiable contribution he might have made to specific reform tactics or to specific reform issues, such as old age pensions or universal suffrage, although it should be noted that when Gladstone argued for universal suffrage in 1864, he was criticised by Disraeli for reviving the doctrine of Tom Paine.[22] While the improvement in the economic lot of the British worker may be attributable in large part to the activities of trade unions, the underlying spirit behind that movement owes its beginnings to Paine. William Cobbett noted in 1822 that Paine had 'awakened ... the spirit of enquiry' in the common man.[23] G.D.H. Cole pointed out that Paine had set on foot 'the first unmistakable movement of working-class radicalism in England'.[24] And this was not just a random, ephemeral eruption. It signalled the development of a new consciousness among working men: an awareness of their rights, a casting off of traditional deference to the upper classes, a discovery that even the worker in the field and factory might assert a claim to human dignity. Such was the larger message underlying the writings of Thomas Paine — a message that went out to thousands of cottages across England, a message kept alive by Cobbett and Richard Carlile, by Holyoake and Bradlaugh, and by dozens of others.

The American revival of interest in Paine had an entirely different history. When William Cobbett fled to America in 1817 to escape possible confinement after the suspension of the Habeas Corpus act, he quite quickly became convinced that Paine had been forgotten by the American public. In January 1818, Cobbett announced that he was going to write

> an account of the Life, Labours and Death of that famous Englishman, Thomas Paine; and, perhaps, to collect and republish the whole of his writings complete in cheap form, and with some explanatory notes to the Rights of Man ... Justice to his memory, justice to the cause of freedom, justice to the country that gave him birth, justice to his friends on both sides of the Atlantic, demand at my hands an earnest endeavour to perform this task in a manner worthy of the subject.[25]

In preparation for this work, Cobbett sought out some of Paine's surviving acquaintances, including Madame de Bonneville, who had been preparing notes for a biography of Paine which Cobbett rewrote but never published. As the manuscript reveals, Cobbett was especially irked to find that Paine had been committed to 'an obscure grave on an open and disregarded bit of land':[26]

> Paine lies in a little hole under the grass and weeds of an obscure farm in America. There, however, *he shall not lie, unnoticed, much longer.* He belongs to England. His fame is the property of England; and if no other people will show that they value that fame, the people of England will.[27]

If that did not make it clear what Cobbett intended, all ambiguity was removed by the appearance of Cobbett in New Rochelle early one morning, accompanied by a wagon, shovels and several friends. Without authority from anyone he proceeded to dig up Paine's coffin, which he took with him when he sailed for England in October 1819.

This single act brought Paine to the attention of a large public on both sides of the Atlantic. Cobbett's purpose was to raise an appropriate monument in England; he even suggested that the one to William Pitt might be replaced by one to Paine. But Cobbett's timing was particularly bad. When he arrived in Liverpool in November 1819 the country was wholly absorbed by the outrageous conduct of the yeomanry involved in the Peterloo Massacre. The reformers who would have been most sympathetic to Paine's claims were occupied in a heated assault on the government. And the ministry was in no mood to tolerate the deification of one of history's greatest revolutionaries. The administration came down hard on Cobbett with the full weight of its powerful press. Cobbett was relentlessly cartooned and ridiculed by poets and would-be poets. Lord Byron, whose aristocratic liberalism would not allow any merit in a pair of lower-class reformers, joined the fun:

> In digging up your bones, Tom Paine,
>   Will Cobbett has done well;
> You visit him on earth again,
>   He'll visit you in hell.[28]

There was no way to raise the money needed for a Paine monument. A public dinner scheduled by Cobbett for 29 January 1820 to celebrate Paine's birthday was cancelled because of the refusal of the landlord to provide accommodations. Cobbett himself was in serious financial difficulties, and found it impossible to fulfil his grandiose plans.[29] On Cobbett's death, 16 years after the bones had landed at Liverpool, they had found no permanent resting place. Cobbett died in 1835 on his farm at Normandy, near Farnham, Surrey. He was bankrupt and the bones were included among his household effects. No one knows exactly what became of them after that. They were rejected as non-assets by the receiver who auctioned off Cobbett's goods. In the ensuing century and a half all sorts of conjectures have been put forward. The surviving heirs of Cobbett believe that the bones were buried some years past in the garden of one of the members of the family. Perhaps it is not inappropriate that both Paine and Burke, the chief antagonists in the battle over the principles of the French Revolution, have unidentified final resting places.

Possibly because of the stir caused by Cobbett's body-snatching, or, more probably, because of the Paine renaissance in England sparked by Richard Carlile's publications, an edition of Paine's theological works was published in New York in 1821, the first in more than 25 years. Three years later came a Boston edition of the political works. It had been 20 years since anyone in Boston (or any other city in America) had deemed it suitable to reprint *Common Sense* or *Rights of Man*. The Boston edition was suitably deferential to American sensibilities. It omitted Paine's *Letter to Washington*, because it was believed to have been written during a time of great irritation of mind, occasioned by his imprisonment, while in France, and from a misconception of the motives which induced Washington to refrain from interfering to obtain his release'.[30] And although the edition purported to be limited to Paine's 'political writings', the publisher felt it necessary to include an apology for his *Age of Reason*: 'There is nothing to palliate it; nor one good argument that can be urged in its favor.'

This native timidity towards Paine's religious writings was more than offset by the efforts of a number of English free-thinkers who travelled to America at this time — some as visitors, others as emigrants — all intoxicated with the spirit of the Paine revival that had swept England a half dozen years before. There was, for example, George Houston, who had been imprisoned in Newgate for two years for his involvement in the translation and publication of d'Holbach's *Ecce Homo*. Houston came to America around 1820. By 1822 he was publishing *The Minerva* in New York and in 1827 he started *The Correspondent*, one of the early freethought journals published in America. He also assisted in editing *The Correspondent* by another English emigrant, the youthful George Henry Evans (1805-55).[31] Better known to history than either Houston or Evans was Robert Owen (1771-1858), father of English socialism, who was the principal owner of the largest cotton spinning mill in Britain. Owen came to America in 1824 to establish a model community at New Harmony,

Indiana. By 1825 the religious writings of Paine were being taught in the New Harmony schools. Paine's birthday became an annual celebration there and similar parties were initiated in New York in 1825, spreading to other major cities throughout the country, and continuing throughout the century.[32] George Macdonald claimed that he had attended these gatherings for more than 50 years between 1876 and 1928.[33]

The famous, or infamous, Frances Wright (1795-1852), a young Scottish radical and admirer of Paine, who came to America in 1824 and who later bore Owen's son, Robert Dale Owen, opened a Hall of Science in New York City where lectures on Paine's religious views as well as on women's rights were offered to large audiences. Other Paine disciples among English emigrants included Gilbert Vale (1788-1860), later biographer of Paine, who came to America in 1829, and the self-educated shoe-maker, Benjamin Offen (1772-1848), who had made the trip five years before. Frances Wright was the most notable lecturer of all the newcomers; she created a sensation as she travelled across the country speaking to large audiences in city after city; but the others also lectured and wrote until America was indoctrinated with Paine theories. The interest evoked by their efforts led to a spate of new editions of Paine's works.

Two strains that can be identified with Paine became an indissoluble part of American life. His printed works were frequently among the possessions of people migrating to the western wilderness. Paine represented to them both the spirit of independence (which included contempt for any aristocracy other than one based on merit), and the vision of America as the land of promise and youthful hope, consciously embracing a creed superior to the outworn tyrannies of the old world. 'We have it in our power to begin the world over again' Paine had said in a dozen ways. And this is what the western migration meant to many of the hardy adventurers who made the trip. The cheekiness or even arrogance that the world often sees in Americans was almost certainly a product of this creed.

Paine's writings became the primer of American frontier society in the early nineteenth century. Abraham Lincoln, born in 1809, studied Paine's works as he grew up in a cabin in southern Illinois, as did thousands of other youths in the wilderness.[34] A missionary in Wisconsin wrote in 1841 that 'Paine's Age of Reason is read with avidity and its doctrines are boldly and strenuously advocated by men of influence.' In one Indiana village 40 per cent of the families were openly non-believers in the Scriptures. 'Missouri was regarded as especially partial to freethought.'[35] Paine was said to be 'the most widely read author in early Kentucky;'[36] and Robert Dale Owen, on a lecture tour in the West in 1831, wrote that deism was the most prevalent belief in the United States.[37]

At almost the same time as Paine's doctrines were carried westward, the same doctrines, softened and intellectualised for an educated audience, entered American society through a wholly different route. Although Paine's writings had disappeared from bookshops for two decades after the close of the eighteenth century, they were widely read, perhaps in battered copies, by the students that attended Harvard and many of the other educational institutions that had made the most vigorous efforts to stamp them out. What Paine wrote (and what others had written along the same lines) revolutionised the intellectual life of New England, slowly spreading from there to the rest of the country.

The most obvious example is that afforded by the works of Ralph Waldo Emerson. Emerson graduated from Harvard in 1821 when he was 18 years old. He was licensed to preach in 1826 and three years later became pastor of the Second Unitarian Church in Boston. In 1831 he became 'the first man of high social position in America who openly took the anti-slavery position' — a position which Paine had publicly taken more than fifty years before. At the time when Emerson took his stand, the churches of New England, even in enlightened Boston, were vigorous defenders of slavery, and Emerson and other abolitionists who followed him found it necessary to resign their clerical appointments. But Emerson's break with the church did not end there. In his Divinity School Address at Harvard in 1838, he attacked biblical miracles head on, declaring that 'the word Miracle, as pronounced by Christian churches, gives a false impression'.[38] Earlier he had declared that 'The invariable mark of wisdom is to see the miraculous in the common.'[39] Like Paine he saw God manifested in the Creation of the universe: 'All science has one aim, namely to find a theory of nature.'[40] Men should behold God and Nature face to face in an original relation to the universe, not through church writings: 'wise men pierce this rotten diction.'[41] The student must not become 'The parrot of other men's thinking'; each age must write its own books; men can read God directly in Nature.[42]

Paine had said that 'Practical religion consists in doing good; and the only way of serving God is that of endeavoring to make His Creation happy.'[43] Emerson wrote that man is born to do good; only when he serves virtue 'is the end of the creation answered, and God ... well pleased'.[44] Man's duty is a moral one, he should serve his fellow man rather than worship an abstract deity: 'There are innocent men', Emerson wrote, 'who worship God after the tradition of their fathers, but their sense of duty has not yet extended to the use of all their faculties.'[45]

Paine had said that 'Jesus wrote no account of himself' — 'his historians having brought him into the world in a supernatural manner, were obliged to take him out in the same manner.'[46] Emerson declared that 'Historical Christianity has fallen into the error that corrupts all attempts to communicate religion ... It has dwelt, it dwells, with noxious exaggeration about the *person* of Jesus.'[47] Emerson foresaw a 'new church founded on moral science ... the next age will behold God in the ethical laws ... heeding no prophet'.[48]

Emerson, like Paine, hailed the age of revolution: he extolled the rise of individualism and welcomed greater equality: 'the movement that elevated the lower class brought out the study of the man, the low, the common, as contrasted with the sublime and beautiful'. Surely these latter words — the title of the essay that first brought Burke to public attention — were intended by Emerson to fly in the face of Burke's attempt to deify the upper classes.[49] It might also be more than coincidence that Emerson's enthusiasm for manmade structures using forms from nature (for example, Smeaton's Eddystone lighthouse, Dolland's telescope and Duhmal's bridge)[50] paralleled Paine's thoughts for his iron bridge: 'I took the idea ... from a spider's web', said Paine, 'and I naturally supposed that when nature enabled that insect to make a web, she taught it the best method of putting it together.'[51]

Emerson's Divinity School Address of 1838 so infuriated

the Harvard faculty that he was not invited back until 1866. Paine's name does not appear in the Address, nor in any of Emerson's talks or essays, but Emerson's notes confirm that he read Paine, as could be assumed of any educated person of the time. Emerson's private musings credit Paine with good intentions and with having helped humanity by resisting the overpowering tendency of Christianity to 'absorb the race'.[52] Despite Emerson's opinion that Paine had been too forthright, and despite his reluctance to mention names, Samuel Ripley, Emerson's half-uncle and one of his close friends, recognised the Paine influence in the Address, even if no one else did. In a letter to Emerson written shortly after the talk, Ripley pleaded with Emerson not to publish it: 'the world needs to be enlightened — but I don't want to see you classed with Kneeland, Paine & co., bespattered & belied.'[53] Abner Kneeland (1774-1844) was not only an outspoken admirer of Paine, but he was openly intimate with Robert Dale Owen and Frances Wright, who were then bringing Paine's religious views to the attention of audiences across America. Kneeland had been convicted of blasphemy in 1835, for which he served a 60-day prison sentence.[54] And in 1837, the year before Emerson's Divinity School Address, Kneeland had published an edition of *The Age of Reason* in Boston.

The Divinity School Address *was* published, and Emerson's views became a part of polite Christian tradition among the more liberal churches. They also became one of the channels by which the intellectuals of America were indoctrinated with freethought philosophy.[55] Even during Emerson's lifetime, Unitarian churches began to acknowledge an affinity with Paine. A typical expression of the emerging reception to Paine's views is found in the diary of the great Harvard zoologist, E.S. Morse, who wrote in 1859, when he was 21 years old:

> I have been reading Thomas Paine's 'Age of Reason' and instead of finding it the gross writings of a low mind I found a writer who held a high and holy opinion of God, whose death was mild and serene, contrary to the Pious Frauds circulated from the Pulpit.[56]

That one can be too honest for one's own good was the

lesson inherent in the fate of Paine. More practical men have followed the advice of Montaigne: 'I speak the truth', he wrote, 'not enough to satisfy myself, but as much as I dare speak.'[57] The demand or intellectual conformity that was exerted upon American thinkers during the early years of the nineteenth century is silently disclosed in John Marshall's *Life of Washington*. The first edition, published in 1804, contained a long paragraph in praise of Paine's *Common Sense*. A later edition, published in 1833, omitted this paragraph entirely.[58] Early in the current century John M. Robertson spelled out the pressures applied to freethinkers of the past, from Franklin and Washington on to Paine and his successors. Robertson observed these pressures in his own day: American 'social conditions impose on public men the burden of concealment', and this is most apparent where 'commercialism is most stringent'.[59]

It is not a long step from Emerson to his great admirer and younger contemporary, Walt Whitman. At a Thomas Paine birthday ceremony in Philadelphia in 1877, Whitman praised the 'most precious service' rendered to the country by Paine — one of her good and faithful men' — poetically adding that 'I for one ... throw my pebble on the cairn of his memory'.[60]

What has been termed 'The Golden Age of Freethought' in America,[61] the period from 1860 to 1900, was dominated by a single figure: Robert G. Ingersoll (1833-99), one of the ablest orators in American history. While Ingersoll earned a reputation as an outstanding trial lawyer, he was tirelessly lecturing on freethought to enormous audiences throughout the United States. 'No other freethinker, it is believed, has reached such audiences by public speech'.[62] Ingersoll's religious views were derived principally from Paine, who he described as 'one of the greatest of all benefactors of the human race'.[63]

What can one offer as a summary picture of the America shaped by this history? One thing seems certain: America is a country formed of many strands — often inconsistent and hence confusing — but perhaps inevitable in a land with such a great mixture of peoples and living experiences. Clearly identifiable, however, is a strong strand of republicanism, individualism, egalitarianism, self-confidence and belief in progress that echoes Paine's belief that we can begin the world over again. It is a strand that sets America apart, being found nowhere in the world to the same extent; and it remains strong enough to survive the series of national disappointments of the latter half of the current century. But Paine would be disappointed (and probably greatly surprised) to find another large strand of extreme fundamentalism in religion, widely distributed through the country, existing side by side with the first strand, and not always separated from the first. The second strand, too, may be unique to America among Western nations, at least in its extent and intensity. At the same time there is a substantial strand of religious rationalism in America, mostly unorganised, uncountable, and submerged, that quietly and vaguely represents the views of Thomas Paine, sometimes as modified by Emerson and his followers (as in the case of the Unitarians and Universalists), but more often without anything approaching a church or creed, or even those general concepts expressed by Paine himself. Among them can be counted atheists, deists, agnostics and freethinkers.

Thus Paine left America a mixed heritage that accepts him (although often hesitatingly) as a founder and patriot, but is embarrassed by his religious views, which the majority of Americans fail to understand. Theodore Roosevelt, twenty-sixth president of the United States, once referred to Paine as a 'filthy little atheist', without having studied the subject.[64] The marble bust of Paine by Sidney H. Morse, commissioned by a group of citizens for installation in Independence Hall, was rejected by the City of Philadelphia in 1876, accepted in 1905, displayed in Independence Hall from 1905 until 1931, kept in dead storage from 1931 to 1957, and displayed by the Friendship Liberal League in Philadelphia from 1957 to 1967, when it was turned over to the American Philosophical Society on the understanding that it would be kept in the private office of the Society's librarian. The nation's debt to Paine was less ambiguously acknowledged by the decision in 1945 that he should join Washington, Jefferson, Adams and his other great contemporaries in the national Hall of Fame; and some 20 years later, in 1968, when there was issued a new 40-cent postage stamp bearing Paine's picture.[65] Perhaps Ingersoll's comment on Paine, made more than 100 years ago, is at last being realised:

Thomas Paine was one of the intellectual heroes — one of the men to whom we are indebted. His name is associated forever with the Great Republic. As long as free government exists he will be remembered, admired and honored.

He lived a long, laborious and useful life. The world is better for his having lived. For the sake of truth he accepted hatred and reproach for his portion. He ate the bitter bread of sorrow. His friends were untrue to him because he was true to himself, and true to them. He lost the respect of what is called society, but kept his own. His life is what the world calls failure and what history calls success.[66]

Notes

1. Based on titles in *The Thomas Paine Collection of Richard Gimbel in the Library of the American Philosophical Society*, comp. Hildegard Stephens (Wilmington, Delaware, 1976). The 'single exception' was an edition of *Common Sense* in 1803.

2. 'It must have been painful to the feelings of every honest man to think that the writings of Mr. Paine ... should have been so near a total extinction as to be found no where for sale, but in a clandestine manner and at an exorbitant price' (Publisher's Preface to editions of 1817-18, *The Political and Miscellaneous Works of Thomas Paine* (London: R. Carlile, 1819)). See *The Autobiography of Francis Place, 1771-1854*, ed. Mary Thale (Cambridge: Cambridge University Press, 1972), p. 169. In 1816 Cobbett wrote that 'Paine's work is sought after with avidity, at almost any price' (PR, 15 June 1816, p. 751).

3. Quoted in Adrienne Koch (ed.) *Adams and Jefferson: 'Posterity Must Judge'* (Chicago: Rand McNally, 1963), p. 37. *The Anti-Jacobin Review and Magazine* for March 1800 (vol. V, p. 357) reported that the American government had fallen into such decrepitude and disrepute that a 'speedy dissolution' could be expected.

4. 'Infidel societies [in America] had been in existence during the widespread irreligious period after the revolution, but after the death of Elihu Palmer (1806) they disappeared from the scene' (Albert Post, *Popular Freethought in America, 1825-1850* (New York: Columbia University Press, 1943), p. 75).

5. G. Adolph Koch, *Republican Religion; the American Revolution and the Cult of Reason* (1933) (Reprint: Gloucester Mass.: Peter Smith, 1964), p. 168. The feeling against Paine in America was so strong at the time of his death in 1809 that his admirer and friend Joel Barlow wrote that 'this is not the moment to publish the life of that man in this country' (G. Vale, *A Compendium of the Life of Thomas Paine* (New York, 1837), p. 30).

6. E.P. Thompson, *The Making of the English Working Class* (1963) (Harmondsworth: Penguin, 1968), pp. 45-50. See Eric Hobsbawm,

'Methodism and the Threat of Revolution', *History Today*, vol. II, no. 2 (February 1957).

7. *The Courier* was acquired by Daniel Stuart in 1799. Under the guidance of its editor, Peter Street, it became 'the chief ministerial organ in the London press' (H.R. Fox-Bourne, *English Newspapers* (London: Chatto and Windus, 1887), vol. I, p. 275). For the *True Briton* and *Sun*, see Arthur Aspinall, *Politics and the Press, 1780-1850* (London: Home and Van Thal, 1949), p. 78.

8. *Anti-Jacobin Review and Magazine*, vol. X, p. 98.

9. Ibid., vol. VII, p. 194, 434; vol. IX, pp. 26-7, 51, 188, 518; vol. X, pp. 40, 285, 394, 307.

10. PR, 2 May 1812, p. 545.

11. PR, 9 November 1811, p. 583.

12. Jose de Onis, *The United States as Seen by Spanish-American Visitors, 1776-1890* (1952) (New York: Gordian Press, 1975), p. 37.

13. PR, 13 June 1812, p. 748. Almost certainly Cobbett had read *The Age of Reason* at an earlier date. In 1796 he had written an article condemning it, followed by another critical article a year later (see *Porcupine's Works* (London 1801), vol. III, p. 389, vol. VI, p. 80). These articles were reprinted in a small pamphlet in 1819 entitled 'Observations on Thomas Paine and his Age of Reason by William Cobbett'.

14. For examples see PR, 25 September 1813, p. 390; 11 February 1815, p. 170; 20 January 1816, p. 76; 4 May 1816, p. 566; 15 June 1816, p. 751; 17 August 1816, p. 217; 9 November 1816, p. 582. As early as 1810, Cobbett acknowledged Paine's 'very great and rare talents as a writer', adding that he had previously 'been one of his most violent assailants' (PR, 7 November 1810, pp. 842-3n.).

15. Gwyn Williams, 'General Editor's Preface' to Edward Royle, (ed.) *The Infidel Tradition from Paine to Bradlaugh* (London: Macmillan, 1976), p. xi.

16. See two books by Edward Royle: *Victorian Infidels: The Origins of the British Secularist Movement 1791-1866* (Manchester: Manchester University Press, 1974); *Radicals, Secularists and Republicans: Popular Freethought in Britain* (Manchester: Manchester University Press, 1980).

17. Royle (ed.), *The Infidel Tradition*, p. xvii. The Secular societies were maintaining the birthday party traditions of the Chartists — see Dorothy Thompson, *The Chartists* (New York: Pantheon, 1984), p. 150.

18. Hypathia Bradlaugh Bonner, *Charles Bradlaugh: A Record of His Life and Work* (London: T. Fisher Unwin, 1902), vol. I, p. 378n.

19. Royle (ed.), *The Infidel Tradition*, p. 70.

20. Royle, *Radicals, Secularists and Republicans*, pp. 167-8. 'The National Secular Society, which always regarded *The Age of Reason* as a main agent of conversion, printed an edition of sixty thousand copies in 1937 which was sold out in two years': Susan Budd, *Varieties of Unbelief: Atheists and Agnostics in English Society, 1850-1960* (London: Heinemann, 1977), p. 107.

21. Robert Louis Stevenson, *The Amateur Emigrant*, in *The Works of Robert Louis Stevenson* (London: Chatto and Windus, 1909), vol. II, p. 71.

22. George Edinger and E.J.C. Neep, *The Grand Old Man: A Gladstone Spectrum* (London: Methuen, 1936), p. 153.

23. PR, 21 December 1822, p. 707.

24. G.D.H. Cole, *A Short History of the British Working-Class Movement* (London: George Allen and Unwin, 1925-7), vol. I p. 46. See also G.M. Trevelyan, *Lord Grey of the Reform Bill* (London: Longmans, Green, 1920), p. 42: 'the Tom Paine movement re-emerged in the days of Peterloo as the radical creed of the working man in Lancashire and the industrial north'.

25. PR, 24 January 1818, p. 128.

26. Conway, *Paine*, vol. II, pp. 430, 455.

27. PR, 18 September 1819, pp. 131-2.

28. Thomas Moore, *The Life, Letters and Journals of Lord Byron* (London: John Murray, 1908), p. 432.

29. PR, 22 January 1820, p. 709; 27 January 1820, p. 775. Albert Post claims that a birthday celebration for Paine was held 'secretly' in London in 1818 (Post, *Popular Freethought*, pp. 75n., 155). Edward Royle refers to such a party in Leeds in 1822 (Royle, *Victorian Infidels*, p. 36).

30. The title-page indicates 'Charleston, Ms.', now part of Boston, as the place of publication. At p. xii the editor states that 'It is well known that the critical situation of our efforts at the time, both with England and France, precluded the possibility of intervening in his behalf, without endangering the peace of the country.' Still, this does not adequately explain why Washington did not at least send personal well-wishes to Paine.

31. Emigration brought to America a number of Paine disciples: see Post, *Popular Freethought*; Marshall Brown and Gordon Stein, *Freethought in the United States: A Descriptive Bibliography* (Westport, Conn.: Greenwood, 1978); J.F.C. Harrison, *Quest for the New Moral World: Robert Owen and the Owenites in Britain and America* (New York: Charles Scribner, 1969); Koch, *Republican Religion*.

32. The deistic papers published in America during Paine's lifetime included *The Temple of Reason* (1800-3) and *Prospect*, or *View of the Moral World* (1803-5). In 1810 a few Paine followers began *The Theophilanthropist* which lasted for only nine issues (Koch, *Republican Religion*, pp. 84, 92-3, 104, 106). Regarding *The New Harmony Gazette*, and its successors, published by Robert Dale Owen and Frances Wright, see Brown and Stein, *Freethought in the United States*.

33. George E. Macdonald, *Fifty Years of Freethought in America* (New York: Truth Seeker Co., 1929), vol. I, p. 176.

34. Kunigunde Duncan and D.P. Nickols, *Mentor Graham: The Man who Taught Lincoln* (Chicago: The University of Chicago Press, 1944), pp. 143-4.

35. Post, *Popular Freethought*, p. 189.

36. William Garrett West, *Barton Warren Stone: Early American Advocate of Christian Unity* (Nashville, Tenn.: Disciples of Christ Historical Society, 1954), p. 22.

37. Post, *Popular Freethought*, p. 193.

38. Bliss Perry (ed.), *Selections from the Prose Writings of Ralph Waldo Emerson* (Boston: Houghton Mifflin, 1926), p. 82.

39. 'Nature' (1836), in ibid., p. 53.

40. Ibid., p. 14.

41. Ibid., p. 28.

42. 'The American Scholar' (1837), in ibid., p. 57.

43. English Preface to *Agrarian Justice*, in *Writings*, vol. I, p. 609.

44. Perry, (ed.) *Emerson*, p. 77. See also 'Nature', p. 34: 'a thing is good only so far as it serves'.

45. 'Nature', in ibid., p. 53.

46. *The Age of Reason*, in *Writings*, vol. I, p. 468.

47. 'Divinity School Address', in Perry (ed.), *Emerson*, pp. 82-3.

48. Emerson, quoted in Edwin S. Mead, 'Emerson's Ethics', in F.B. Sanborn (ed.), *The Genius and Character of Emerson* (Boston: J.R. Osgood, 1885), pp. 245-6.

49. 'Divinity School Address', pp. 82-3 .

50. [Moncure D. Conway], 'The Culture of Emerson', *Fraser's Magazine*, vol. LXXVIII (July 1868), p. 8.

51. Paine to George Staunton, 1789, *Writings*, vol. II, p. 1044.

52. Merton M. Sehets, Jr (ed.), *The Journals and Miscellaneous Notebooks of Ralph Waldo Emerson* (Cambridge, Mass.: Belknap Press, 1965), vol. V, p. 202; vol. IX, p. 12. Emerson declined an invitation to speak on Paine to a London audience, ibid., vol. IV, p. 12.

53. Ralph Rusk (ed.), *The Letters of Ralph Waldo Emerson* (New York: Columbia University Press, 1939), vol. I, p. 148n.

54. Arthur M. Schlesinger Jr, *The Age of Jackson* (Boston: Little, Brown, 1945), pp. 356-8.

55. Emerson's followers refused to acknowledge Paine. In 1885, Edwin Mead, one of Emerson's disciples, declared that the Harvard Divinity Address of 1838 was 'the first free and full utterance of rational religion in America' (Mead 'Emerson's Ethics', p. 235).

56. Dorothy G. Wayman, *Edward Sylvester Morse: A Biography* (Cambridge, Mass.: Harvard University Press, 1942), pp. 52-3.

57. *The Essays of Montaigne*, trans. E.J. Trechman (New York: Oxford University Press, 1946), vol. II, p. 259.

58. John Marshall, *Life of Washington* (Philadelphia: C.P. Wayne, 1804), vol. II, p. 399; ibid. (Philadelphia: J. Crissy, 1833), vol. I, pp. 76-7.

59. John M. Robertson, *A Short History of Freethought, Ancient and Modern*, second edition (New York: G.P. Putnam, 1906), vol. II, pp. 408, 410.

60. Whitfield J. Bell Jr, *The Bust of Thomas Paine* (Philadelphia: American Philosophical Society, 1974), pp. 14-15.

61. Brown and Stein, *Freethought in the United States*, p. 47.

62. Robertson, *Freethought, Ancient and Modern*, vol. II, p. 336.

63. Eva Ingersoll (ed.), *The Letters of Robert G. Ingersoll* (Wakefield, N.Y.: Philosophical Library, 1951), p. 50.

64. Theodore Roosevelt, *Gouverneur Morris* (New York: Houghton Mifflin, 1888), p. 289. The Conway archives at Columbia University contain extensive correspondence between Roosevelt and W.M. Van der Weyde regarding the remark. See also Elting E. Morison (ed.), *The Letters of Theodore Roosevelt* (Cambridge, Mass.: Harvard University Press, 1954), vol. VIII, p. 1309; Marilla M. Ricker, 'A Square Deal' (New York: Vincent Parke, 1908), vol. I, p. 342.

65. See Bell, *Bust of Thomas Paine, passim*.

66. From a talk at Fairburg, Illinois, in 1871: *Life and Writings of Thomas Paine*, ed. Wheeler, vol. I, p. 309.

Index

149